The Spirit of Bead Embroidery

The Spirit of Bead Embroidery

by Heidi Kummli

KB
KALMBACH BOOKS

Kalmbach Books
21027 Crossroads Circle
Waukesha, Wisconsin 53186
www.Kalmbach.com/Books

Published in 2012
16 15 14 13 12   1 2 3 4 5

Manufactured in the United States of America

ISBN: 978-0-87116-438-4

Editor: *Karin Van Voorhees*
Art Director: *Lisa Bergman*
Graphic Designer: *Lisa Schroeder*
Photographer: *William Zuback*

Library of Congress Cataloging-in-Publication Data

Kummli, Heidi.
   The spirit of bead embroidery / by Heidi F. Kummli.

   p. : ill. (chiefly col.); cm.

   ISBN: 978-0-87116-438-4

   1. Bead embroidery--Handbooks, manuals, etc. 2. Bead embroidery—
Patterns. 3. Jewelry making—Handbooks, manuals, etc. 4. Four
elements (Philosophy) in art. 5. Decoration and ornament—Animal forms.
I. Title.

NK9302 .K85 2012
746.5

Light Woman's Spirit Bead

By Rose Red Elk-Red Feather Woman

Light Woman anxiously awaited the arrival of the Blue Coats. They would have with them a group of white traders who traveled from the strange land across the waters. She had dealings with the traders, many moons ago. She made leather pouches in exchange for bags of glass beads. She expected them to have more beads, and they did.

Carefully, after bargaining with the white men, she hurried back to her camp to complete her beaded cradle board. Quietly she strung her sinew (thread), caressing the board and placing her design together. As she wove the beads with her thread, she thought of her new grandchild.

With each bead she placed a prayer for the unborn child. Each bead held a prayer for good things to come, protection, well being and a healthy long life. As she strung the beads, she purposely left a color off center, adding an additional bead to the pattern, a spirit bead. A flaw was created.

This flaw communicated to the Great Spirit her humility, proving she was not perfect, nor was her beadwork. The spirit bead was special, the connection to the unseen world where the ancestors live, guiding Light Woman and her people.

In the beginning, the Creator organized and created all living things. As human beings, we come to our Earth Walk and as our spirit enters our body with our first breath, we begin our journey as individual souls.

As our artist ways began to take shape, indigenous people throughout the world began their quest for creating. As a Lakota/Assiniboine woman, and an artist, storyteller, and musician, I began to learn and understand the masters before me—the elders who beaded and bent porcupine quills, made dyes from plants, and traded with the white men for the beads they brought with them from Europe.

It is our way to show humility to the Creator, to show a flaw in our beadwork. It expresses how we know we are not perfect, only the Great Spirit is.

When I first met Rose many moons ago, I felt a sense of power, yet peace as well. When you listen to her sing and tell her stories, you never want to forget them. Rose shares the wisdom of her ancestors for the younger generation but also as a reminder that though we may have grown apart from the teachings of the earth, we still need them—they are deep in each and every one of us. I am honored Rose shared her story of the Spirit Bead. May we all be so humble and acknowledge our own imperfections. —H.K.

Contents

Foreword

It is my honor to write this foreword.

Years ago, I was browsing through a magazine and a piece of beadwork caught my attention and took my breath away. It was an elaborate collar with pearls cascading from turquoise cabochons. The beaded piece spoke to me like no other had ever before. I was enamored with it. Many years later, I entered a competition and won a finalist position. One of the other finalists was Heidi Kummli, the artist I had long admired. I was more thrilled to meet this fabulous artist than worry about an award, which by the way, Heidi won a deserved first place. We choose to sit together at the ceremony and have been friends ever since. It was a true meeting of two souls that connected in ways that no words can describe.

The Spirit of Bead Embroidery defines the spirit behind beaded art and explores the stones used in this artform. While everyone who creates does so from their own hearts, this book leads you through the fascinating meanings behind stones, animals, and natural elements. Since reading Heidi's words, I have found myself observing nature in a much more appreciative and meaningful way. This book embraces the spirituality of beadwork and the beautiful soul of the dear artist who has written it. From front to back, the book is overflowing with inspiration from images of Heidi's fine beadwork and beautifully created projects.

Heidi's Native American heritage is her influence. She embraces her roots and shares her knowledge and with us. Heidi's spirit can be felt on every page, making this the most beautiful book I have ever owned.

Thank you, Heidi, for your beautiful spirit.

—Sherry Serafini

Introduction

Whether I'm sitting on a mountaintop or sitting at my desk beading, a feeling of healing peace and tranquility flows through me. My spirit is at one with the universe and with the beads.

We all have a journey here on earth: a unique path; a lesson to learn; beliefs to uncover. When my path led me to breast cancer in 2007, at first I was devastated, and then I realized it was one of life's many lessons—a gift. The small things in life didn't matter so much, nor did the big ones. Being conscious of the moment we find ourselves in right now, rather than focusing on the future and past, helps us eliminate pain, suffering, and possibly even illness. During my chemotherapy treatments, I was able to do my beadwork, and found the process had a meditative and healing quality. Living in the mountains and being close to nature also makes me feel this way. You may think that if you live in a city you may not be close to nature, but you are nature—look at your hands and feet and feel the air in your lungs. Look at the sun outside the window or the wood of the chair you sit in; nature is all around you.

I hope this book connects you to the natural and spiritual world. It begins with an overview of tools, supplies, and stitches to get you going in bead embroidery and loomwork. Next, you'll find inspirational pages about animal totems, healing stones, colors, and the four elements. Use this information to find your own spirit and inner peace, and think about the animal totems and healing stones you'll use in your jewelry. The 12 projects I created for this book are just a small sampling of what is possible. They are here for you to learn and are a starting point in this journey. The projects begin with the easiest and work their way up to more difficult. At the beginning of each project, I've provided design notes. I tell you how I made my material choices and ask you some questions that may help you make yours. Follow my directions literally, or personalize your jewelry with stones, colors, and totems that are important to you. After my projects you'll find a contribution from Sherry Serafini—a very special woman in our world. The book closes with a beautiful gallery of inspirational and spiritual beaded art from amazing artists that is sure to transform you.

The necklaces pictured on this page are my own. I wear the owl every day because owl is one of my totems. The carved beach stone and frog necklace I wore through my chemotherapy treatments; it is my healing and cleansing piece. The bone wolf necklace is my special occasion necklace for power and confidence. The wolf in this piece looks very much like my dog, Timber, so I like him close to my heart. I hope that you, too, can feel, hear, and reflect the beauty of your surroundings and make yourself or someone you love a special totem amulet—a piece that will bring beauty and peace into your world today and for generations to come.

Peacefully,
Heidi F. Kummli

spírít

noun

1 the nonphysical part of a person that is the seat of emotions and character; the soul: *We seek a harmony between body and spirit.* Such a part regarded as a person's true self and as capable of surviving physical death or separation: *A year after he left, his spirit is still present.*

— Webster's II New Riverside Dictionary

Techniques
Tools • Supplies • Tips • Stitches

Tools are amazing and helpful. They have been around for millions of years. The first humans made tools from stones, flint, bone, and other materials they had available. By using a harder material, they were able to put holes into softer materials such as shells, stones, or bone: the first beads. By using a small animal bone with a hole drilled on one end and a sharp point on the other, they were able to push sinew through leather in an easier and more efficient way: A needle was born.

While tools have evolved over many years, I still like the idea of making tools out of items we may have lying around. The tools in the following pages are used for bead embroidery and loomwork. Some you can find at your local bead or craft store, and others are easily made with items you may have already.

Indigenous people all over the world have used animal hides as embroidery foundation and tree saps and other natural components for glues. You don't need many supplies for bead embroidery or loomwork. That's the magic of beadwork: The supplies are minimal and small. Beading supplies have come a long way in the past two decades—or should one say, millions of years. Though we have progressed with supplies and tools, the art and spirit of beadwork still remains the same: It's a time to reflect and to honor, and the results are always beautiful and transforming.

We can all use a few tips to help our beading. I have selected a few that many students ask or that I feel may help you with bead embroidery and loomwork.

The stitches I use are easy and few; by mastering these, you can accomplish many beautiful results. You'll learn basic backstitch to fill in your background on a larger collar or necklace, edge stitches, bezeling up the side of a cabochon, and how to add depth and texture to your beadwork by tacking down larger beads or twisting a row of beads. Bead loomwork is fun and easy, and in no time you will be making some awesome pieces to share and wear.

I find it incredibly astounding that from the stone age there has not been a time, a culture, or place on the face of the planet that did not have beads! Beads are among the first expression cave dwellers had to invoke, and interact with, their animistic beliefs—our initial protection from the un-understood.

— Jacob March, Nomad Bead Merchants

Tools

Beading Loom

You can find beading looms at most bead or craft stores. They all work well. I prefer a wooden loom instead of a metal loom, although I am sure metal looms also work fine. The wooden looms allow you to use tacks on either end to attach the warp threads. (To read more about looming, see page 20.)

Bead Pad

The bead pad is just that—a place where your beads can hang out and play together. Make your own with an old piece of corrugated cardboard cut to 12x8 in. and covered with Ultrasuede or another type of fabric you like to bead on. Avoid fabric that has fibers sticking up, such as felt, as these will catch on your needle. Also pick a fabric color that is calming to look at and that shows the beads. Corrugated cardboard lining works well because you can stick your needles into it so you won't lose them and it's also stiff enough that you can move the pad around if you want to start another project.

Bead Scoop

The bead scoop is a great tool for picking up your beads or moving them around. You can find some cool metal scoops in many of the bead stores or simply make your own by bending some cardboard and using some tape.

Clothespins

Clothespins are great little clamps to use when you're gluing things together, such as loomwork or bead embroidery to a cuff bracelet.

Crimping Pliers

Use crimping pliers to make a folded crimp to secure beading wire around a clasp on a necklace or bracelet.

Files and Sandpaper

Metal files help with filing down metal parts sticking out that may get in the way of gluing, such as the cut back of a button. Sandpaper also works for flattening the backs of plastic or softer components. Use it to rough up the back of all your cabochons for better adhesion. Coarse 60-grit sandpaper works well.

Fine-Tip Markers

Mark center lines on the foundation to keep the bead embroidery straight and level. Use non-permanent fine-tip markers and remove the lines later with water and a cotton swab. If you use Lacy's Stiff Stuff as a foundation, use a fatter permanent marker (in the same shade as the backing) along the cut edge so it blends in with the backing.

Jeweler's Saw

Jeweler's saws are great for cutting bone or plastic components to create a flat surface for gluing. A vise helps with harder-to-cut materials like bone or wood. Attach leather or Velcro to the jaws so you don't scratch whatever it is you are cutting. Plastic is easier to cut, so you can usually just hold it with your fingers.

Needles

Size 12 beading needles work the best for the projects in this book and for 15º and larger beads. When beading onto Ultrasuede, I prefer #12 sharp beading needles. They are shorter and stronger and don't bend quite as easily as regular #12 beading needles, which may get bent after using them for bead embroidery; use pliers to flatten them out again. The regular #12s are a bit longer than the sharps, and I prefer them for fringes and loomwork. Sometimes, when using smaller beads such as 14ºs, you may want a smaller needle (size 13 or 15). Play with the different needles available and find what works best for you.

Needlenose Pliers

Needlenose pliers work the best for opening and closing jump rings and O-rings when adding a clasp to your necklaces. They also are great for bending earring components and other findings you may need to add to your finished beadwork, and to help pull the needle through a tight bead or thick leather.

Scissors

Get a few different sizes to have on hand and see which ones work best for different tasks. Long scissors work best for making long, clean cuts on Ultrasuede when you want a straight line, and small scissors are great for trimming bead embroidery when you need to get into those tight spaces. Both work fine for trimming cardboard, though the larger scissors are better for thicker cardboard. Cheaper scissors seem to work well for me and I replace them as needed.

Toothpicks

Toothpicks are great for spreading epoxy glue onto cabochons and then cleaning up the excess glue after gluing the cabochons. They are also great for spreading Tacky Glue onto the lining and backing. I use a toothpick with a notch in the end for twisting fringe (see "Fringe" on page 22). I prefer round toothpicks.

Rulers and Compasses

A ruler helps keep your bead embroidery straight and level, especially on larger pieces. It can help you space your stones or other components equally. The compass gives you an even curve when making a collar.

Wire Cutters

Heavy-duty wire cutters come in handy when you need to cut metal elements such as a shank off the back of a button or other components that need removing.

Supplies

Foundation

The foundation is what you will be embroidering your beads upon. Ultrasuede is my first choice. It comes in many colors and thicknesses—the thicker the better. I prefer Ultrasuede Soft. Ultrasuede is easy to get the needle through and doesn't fray when you cut it (which is important in bead embroidery or backing any beadwork because when you add your edging, you don't want it to fray). Lacy's Stiff Stuff is another foundation. It's similar to fabric interfacing, which can be found at your local fabric store. It doesn't fray when cut, is easy to stitch through, and adds thickness. Cabochons glued to it show their true colors because it is white. You can dye Lacy's Stiff Stuff to match your backing or use a marker along the edging to make it blend in. Leather is another choice for foundation, but it is thicker and can be harder to get a needle through.

Backing

All bead embroidery or loomwork needs a backing material. Ultrasuede works great for this because you have many colors to choose from and it also cleans up with soap and water. You can use the same Ultrasuede for your foundation and backing so they match. As with the foundation, you don't want it to fray, so Ultrasuede is perfect. There are many places to get Ultrasuede. Many fabric stores carry it or can special order it (see Resources, page 110).

Lining

Lining lies between the foundation and the backing in bead embroidery. Lining gives your finished beadwork stiffness: The thicker the lining, the stiffer the work. Cardboard lining is the best to use and it's free. Cereal boxes, postcards, or any other kind of cardboard (excluding corrugated) will work. You'll need to line loomwork if you need a stiffer backing, such as for a barrette. Use lightweight cardboard if your loomwork will be used for a cuff bracelet or curved application, such as the Dream Box project (page 72). A fabric interfacing will give loomwork some flexibility. By recycling cardboard, not only are you making your beadwork strong enough to last a lifetime, but you're doing something wonderful for the trees and our Mother Earth.

Beads

As you know, beads come in many colors, sizes, shapes, and attitudes. For bead embroidery, you can use just about any kind you want. The smaller the bead size, the more detail you get. For most of the projects in this book, I use 9º cut gold iris and 15º metallic gold seed beads. I like the metallic golds because they bezel the cabochons so nicely and let the true essence of the stone shine, rather than confusing the eye with other colors. On the other hand, colors can also complement a stone, so play with the bead colors by laying them next to your cabochons to see what looks best. For loomwork, Delicas work the best because they have a uniform size, and they come in a large assortment of colors. Color variation is important because you can achieve gradual shading in a flower or other pattern. You can certainly use smaller beads to get more detail (or larger beads to go faster but with less detail), but keep in mind that you want your beads to be the same size. Otherwise your loomed piece will be lumpy and uneven. By using beads that are matte, shiny, or metallic, you can set them apart from the rest, giving them their own space and message.

Beading Wire

Use beading wire in .021 or .019 diameter for stringing your beaded pendants. You will need a crimp bead on both ends to attach your clasp.

Cabochons

Cabochons are wonderful stones shaped into ovals, circles, or free-form shapes. You can find them at bead stores, online, or at gem and mineral shows. I prefer natural stones. They add life to beadwork along with healing energy. For a few of my favorite vendors, see Resources, page 110.

Cords and Chains

Some of the projects in this book use leather cord. The benefit of cord is that it's a quick and easy way to finish a necklace, either by attaching it to a pendant or using a bail. Leather cord is also very comfortable, especially if it's going to be a piece you will be wearing every day. You can find it in different diameters; 2mm and 4mm work best for me. You can also use metal chains or snake chain. These are comfortable as well and an easy way to finish a piece. If you don't have the time to bead embroider a collar, a chain or cord is a simple solution.

Findings

You will find a large assortment of findings in most craft or bead stores, including clasps, pin backs, earring hooks, and posts. Pick what's comfortable to you and complements your piece. Brass cuffs are great for bracelets and come in different sizes and textures (see Resources, page 110).

Fingernail Polish

Clear fingernail polish secures knots. Use it on the ends of the warp threads in bead looming as well.

Glues

I use two different glues for bead embroidery: Two-part epoxy and Tacky Glue. Two-part epoxy works great for gluing cabochons and most components. You can find many types of epoxy at your hardware or craft store; I like the five-minute

variety so I can get on with my projects. I also use two-part epoxy for gluing post earrings together and attaching findings such as pin backings or end caps on cords. Use rubbing alcohol to clean up two-part epoxy when it's still wet. Once it dries (after about 10 minutes) you will have to use a utility knife to clean it up, so make sure to keep your gluing tidy. Tacky Glue is my favorite glue. It is a user-friendly glue and washes up with water. That said, don't use it on something that will get wet, such as a ring. Use it for gluing linings, backings, and finished bead embroidery or loomwork to cuffs and collars. You can find Tacky Glue at most craft stores (I like the designer Tacky Glue in the pink bottle). Tacky Glue sets after about five minutes, so you can finish your edging. For more about gluing, see "Tips", page 14.

Masking Tape

You'll need masking tape to secure the ends of loomwork. You can also use it to tape additional pieces of Ultrasuede together if you run short when beading. (See tip, page 15.)

Thread

There are many sizes, types, and colors of thread to choose from these days. Nymo size B is what I use for bead embroidery and loomwork. Nymo is available in a large cone which will last a long time. For hand stitching, I like using a dark or a light color depending on the Ultrasuede color I use. If you are doing loomwork, a light color works best because dark thread can change the color of transparent beads and make them less bright. Play with the different kinds of thread available to find what works best for you.

Tips

Threading a Needle

Threading a needle can be a challenge at first, but with practice and patience, you will be threading needles with no problem. Make sure to wet both the thread and the eye of the needle. Cut the thread at an angle. The eye of the needle is actually a bit wider on one side, so it can make a difference which side you pass the thread through; If one side continues to be a problem, try threading the needle from the opposite side. Hold the needle's eye and the thread tip close to your fingertips. If you're still having trouble, try a different needle—sometimes the eye gets plugged.

Making Your Stones Shine

If you glue a clear cabochon to a dark foundation, your stone will become dark as well. To maintain the original color, first glue your cabochon onto aluminum foil using two-part epoxy. Once the glue has dried, trim off the excess foil and proceed with your project.

Don't Throw That Cardboard Out!

Save old cereal boxes and postcards to use for lining on your projects.

Patterns

Needlepoint books are full of great patterns for loomwork because they use the same graph. Make patterns for your collars using old T-shirts: Cut out the collar and use that as a pattern. If you want to embroider an animal, find a simple picture and photocopy it onto a piece of tracing paper temporarily taped to a regular 8½x11-in. sheet. Trim the tracing paper pattern and use rubber cement to glue it to your foundation for beading. See more about this process in the Grace's Angel collar (page 86).

Staying Focused

When working on a large project, sometimes it's hard to stay focused. I like to listen to books on CD. You can borrow them from your local library or purchase downloadable copies from the Internet very easily. I have heard some great books while beading that I would never had the time to read otherwise.

Gluing

It takes a bit of practice to glue cabochons onto the foundation without getting glue all over yourself. First, sand the backs of the cabochons with 60-grit sandpaper. This will help with adhesion. Use a toothpick to mix the two-part epoxy and spread the glue on the back of the stone evenly. More glue is better than not enough—you can always

clean up the excess glue with the toothpick. If the stone is small and hard to handle or hold, use the toothpick with the glue to pick it up and move it to where you want it. Press the stone firmly onto the foundation so the surfaces make a complete bond. Keep your fingers clean with rubbing alcohol, otherwise everything you touch will get sticky and have glue on it. If you get glue on the front of the cabochon, clean it up as well as you can with the alcohol before the glue dries. For gluing linings, use a toothpick to spread Tacky Glue. I find it easier to put the glue on the cardboard lining rather than on the back of the beaded piece.

Maximizing the Healing

Place a small cabochon on the back of your bracelet or necklace. This will truly bring the healing essence of the stone close to you because the stone will touch your skin. Glue a cabochon onto Ultrasuede and backstitch a row or two of beads around it. Trim, and use Tacky Glue to adhere the beaded cabochon to the back of your finished piece.

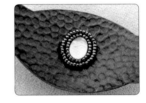

Hiding Knots

To hide a knot while you are stitching edging, place it between the foundation and the backing. To hide a knot on the back of your work, always knot close to the edge. Sew into the Ultrasuede next to the knot and exit ½ in. away, pulling all the tail thread. Trim the tail close to the Ultrasuede.

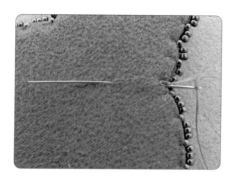

Adding Extra Ultrasuede

Sometimes we need more foundation than we planned for. It's easy to add extra Ultrasuede. Place the working project on some leftover Ultrasuede—a scrap is fine. With a fine tip marker, mark the edge that needs the extension onto the new piece of Ultrasuede. Now cut along the line with scissors. Cut it just big enough for the size Ultrasuede you need. Using some interfacing, measure and cut this about 1-in. wide and long enough for the seam where you will be joining the pieces together. Using Tacky Glue applied with a toothpick, spread the glue on the piece of interfacing. Now lay the project onto half of the interfacing where you need the extension and the new Ultrasuede you just cut on the other half. The seam should almost be invisible. You can embroider right on top and trim as you normally would. Masking tape is a good substitute for interfacing when joining two pieces of Ultrasuede.

Pulling Fringe Taut

Getting your fringe to hang just right can be a challenge, but with practice, this too will become easy and satisfying. With most fringe, you string your beads and go back up through all the beads except for the bottom bead (this bead keeps the thread from coming back out the row of beads). Once you have the needle pushed back up through the row of beads, lay the piece on your work surface. Use your nondominant hand to hold the bottom bead on the table while pulling the thread up towards the top. Keep pulling until the fringe is snug where you want it. As I add fringe along the bottom of my piece, I often pick it up and gently pull on the fringe to get it to hang freely, otherwise the beads have too much tension and don't hang right.

Stitches

Backstitch 4

This is a simple stitch you can use for all kinds of applications. It's great for going around small cabochons or doing detail work. Thread a #12 sharp beading needle with a 2-ft. length of thread and knot one end. Sew up through

the foundation next to a stone or wherever you want to start. Pick up four seed beads, and pull them down to the Ultrasuede, placing them in the direction you want them to go—this could be next to a stone, following a straight line, or wherever your path leads you. Now sew down through the Ultrasuede next to where the fourth bead rests, pulling all the thread and beads down tight to the Ultrasuede. With your needle, sew back up between the second and third bead, and sew through the last two beads. Pick up four more beads, and repeat the process as far as you need to go. After you have gone around the cabochon or finished your row, make sure you sew back through the whole row of beads again. This pulls the row of beads nicely together and straightens it as well. You can add as many rows as you wish. When adding other rows, make sure not to start them too close to the first row or they will bunch up and not lie flat.

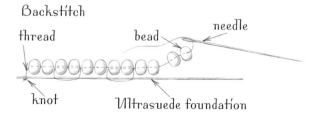

Backstitch 6

Similar to Backstitch 4, this stitch starts with six beads. It works well for beading around larger cabochons and beading longer lines. For Backstitch 6, pick up six beads, sew down next to the sixth bead, sew up between the third and fourth bead, and sew through

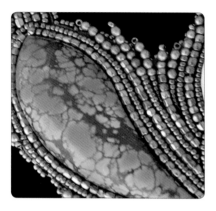

the last three beads. As in Backstitch 4, always go back through your rows when you are finished.

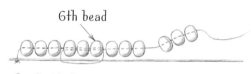

Simple Edging

You can use this simple edging on all your projects. Once your project is glued and trimmed you're ready for edging. Thread a #12 sharp beading needle with a 2-ft. length of thread and knot one end. Sewing between the foundation and the

backing, bring the needle up through the top of the Ultrasuede about $1/16$ in. from the edge (this will hide the knot). Pick up four beads, pull them down next to the Ultrasuede, and sew back up through the backing and foundation about $1/8$ in. over from where you started. Sew back up through the bottom of the fourth or last bead and pull the beads snug. Pick up three beads this time, and again sew down about ⅛ in. from your last stitch and back up through the bottom of the third or last bead. Repeat this process all along the edge. Add or omit beads as needed or as desired. The more beads used, the lacier it looks. Once you reach the starting point, add the required number of beads and go back down through the first bead strung and the backing. Tie a knot and go through the backing about 1 in. from the edge. Come out through the backing and cut the excess thread.

Slanted Edging

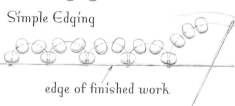

Simple Edging

edge of finished work

This edging is great where you really want a heavy and bold edge. Start by sewing in the edge between the foundation and the backing and bring the needle up through the top of the Ultrasuede about ¹⁄₁₆ in. from the edge (this will

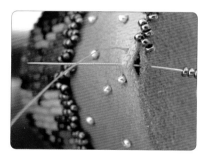

hide the knot). Pick up three 15° seed beads and sew through the Ultrasuede backing and foundation about ⅛ in. from where the needle first came out. Pull the thread and beads snug, pick up three more beads, and continue the slanted edging. Keep the needle placement spaced every ⅛ in. Adjust the spacing based on the size beads you use because larger beads will need to be spaced further apart.

Slanted Edging

Web Bezel

Webbing is great for beading up the side of a tall cabochon or centerpiece. Start by sewing your first row of beads using Backstitch 4 or 6. Step up through a bead in the first row and then add three or five beads. Always use an odd number of beads so you have a middle bead to add another row. After picking up three or five beads, skip two beads in the previous row and sew through the next bead. Pick up three or five beads, skip two beads, and sew through the next. Continue all around your stone or row of beads (you may need to adjust the number of beads toward the end). Bring the needle up through the second or middle bead of one of the three beads just added. Again, you can add three or five beads here. If this is going to be your final row, I recommend adding only three beads as this will bring your beadwork tight to the stone. Go through the last row with your thread to help pull everything snug and straighten the row. If you want to continue the rows of webbing you can continue as before: By adding and omitting beads you can go around unusual cabochons and shapes—be creative here. Use different sizes or colors of beads to give the bezel color and texture.

Web Bezel

Tacking and Anchoring

To anchor unusually shaped beads and focal pieces with thread, find a crevice in the piece, or if it's a bead, sew it down. You can also drill holes if needed—sometimes glue isn't enough and you don't want to

lose that special treasure. If the thread will be visible, string some beads and then sew the object down—this adds to the design. Tacking beads down changes the whole look of the bead. For example, a bead that would be strung horizontally can be used vertically achieving a totally different look. The drawing below presents a few different ways of tacking daggers, bugles, and other beads to your foundation. Give your piece dimension by tacking and anchoring beads and objects; cluster them together to make your beaded piece come alive.

Tacking and Anchoring

Twisting

Twisting a row of beads can add life to your beadwork. If you want a three-dimensional look, crazy hair, or flowing lines, add some twisted beads. When twisting, add more beads on the row than you think you need because

twisting them will shorten the row. Start by sewing up where you want the twist to start. Pick up 30 beads and sew back down through the second-to-last bead. Pick up 28 beads. Sew back down through the foundation next to the first row and pull the beads snug. With the needle, sew back up through the first row of beads and out the last stop bead, pulling the thread. Using the needle, push the tip into the last stop bead. Don't go all the way through the bead but use the needle to twist both rows of beads. Once you get the desired tightness or twist, sew down into the foundation where you want the strand to lie. After you have gotten the hang of it, you can make your rows as long or as short as you want. If you have a really long twisted row, you may want to tack it to the beaded foundation so it doesn't flop around. Add your twist on top of your beadwork rather than a blank foundation; the idea is to bring fullness to your piece.

Twisting

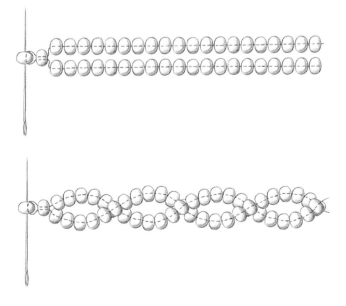

Filling Backgrounds

Students ask me all the time how to complete the backgrounds of their pieces, so I will share three different ways to fill between cabochons or beadwork and make the stones pop. I have used the same odd shape to give you an idea of how the three different backgrounds can work in an uneven world. It also helps to have smaller beads the same color to fit into those small places. Use Backstitch for the backgrounds below.

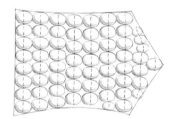 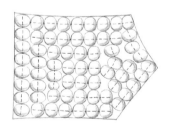 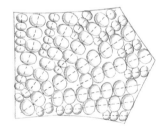

Straight Background

This background follows the lines of a main cabochon, centerpiece or just a line you have added. The lines continue throughout the design. Be careful not to crowd the rows or they will buckle.

Blocking Background

Use this background to fill a space with either the same color or fade the colors of each row to give a shaded effect. Start with a row around each side. End the row with each side; don't form a continuous line. The rows will get smaller and smaller until you're in the middle with only a few beads. If you're shading, the colors could get darker or lighter in the middle.

Fanning Background

If you like an unusual background with different sizes of beads, fanning is your choice. From a corner, draw out some lines—start with the middle line, and then make a line in between the first line and the cabochon or center piece. Use smaller beads to fill in the smaller places.

Loomwork

Loomwork is easy to learn and the only tool you'll need beyond your basic beading setup is a loom. The loomwork projects in this book use a simple loom available at bead or craft stores. Loomwork is very meditative as you get in a rhythm of counting and weaving. I also find that loomwork is done best at your desk rather than on your lap as you can sometimes do with bead embroidery, because of the different color beads and the counting. Delica beads work best for looming because of their consistent size, but any bead will work as long as the size is the same throughout the piece. Patterns for bead looming are the same as needlepoint, so you can find great patterns online. Start with something simple like the Peace Necklace on page 68.

A

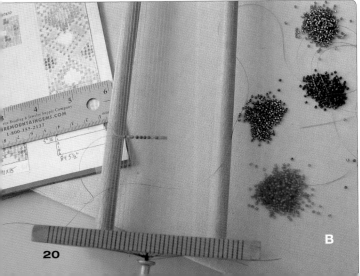

B

Warping your Loom

Warp threads are the threads that run lengthwise and are attached to the ends of the loom. Most looms come with a way to anchor warp threads on each end of the loom. I use a removable tack. The warp threads remain on the loom and are what the weaving threads and beads are woven to. If the row of beads is going to be nine beads wide you will have 10 warp threads—always one more than the number of beads in a row. I place my spool of thread on the floor when I warp my loom because the thread flows off the spool better. Tie the end of your thread (which is still attached to the spool) around one of the tacks or anchors. Tape the tail onto the loom for security **(A)**. Pull the thread through one of the grooves on the loom to the left of the center and through a groove on the opposite side directly across from it, around the tack, and into the next groove. Cross again to the opposite side and around the tack. Repeat until you have the correct number of warp threads for your project. After you have the correct number of warp threads, wrap the thread around the closest tack a few times and tape or tie the end to the loom.

Weaving

Thread 3 ft. of thread on a #12 beading needle. Tie the thread to the warp thread on the left of the loom leaving a 2-in. tail. (If you are left handed, tie on the right side.) Start the row at the bottom of the loom about 2 in. from the side. Pass the weaving thread under the warp threads with the needle and thread exiting the right side. Photo **B** shows how I lay out my workspace: I place the pattern and a guide ruler on the left and beads on the right for easy picking.

Follow the pattern and pick up the number and colors of beads you need for the first row. Pull the beads all the way down to the knot under the warp threads. With your left hand, push the beads up between the warp threads. This may take a little time but once you get the first and second row done, the beads in subsequent rows will just pop into place. Bring the needle around the last warp thread, and go back through the beads **(C)**. Make sure the needle goes on top of the warp threads or your beads will hang loose—you will be able to tell. After the needle is through, pull the row snug. (The first row won't stay tight until you place the second row.) Weave the second row as the first, following the second row on the pattern, pushing the beads up from the bottom, and coming back through from the top. Now you should be able to tighten the two rows. Don't over tighten—just make the beads snug. As you move along, weave the tail in with the left warp thread **(D)** or thread it through a row of beads to hide it. Continue with the pattern. When you run out of thread, tie the end to the left warp thread, hide the tail in a row of beads, and trim the excess thread. To add a new thread, tie it onto the left warp thread as in the beginning. Weave until the pattern is complete.

Taping

That wasn't so bad was it? Now let's get the work off the loom. Using clear fingernail polish, brush the warp threads and knots to help secure everything. While the polish is still tacky, tape the ends with masking tape. Cut a piece of tape a little wider than the loomwork and tape it to the bottom of the warp threads. Fold the ends over the loomwork, keeping the width of the taped section a bit narrower than the loomwork. Trim the ends. Don't push the tape right up to the beads—keep it 1–2mm away **(E)** so the tape folds under the loomwork nicely and you won't see it. After the ends are taped you're ready to cut the loomwork off the loom. Leave ½ in. of tape on the loomwork and when it's free, lay it on a flat surface, and press the tape flat to secure with a small ruler or pencil.

Finishing

To finish, cut a piece of poster board 2mm smaller than the actual loomwork, and use Tacky Glue to adhere it to the back. I put the glue onto the poster board rather than the loomwork. Use Tacky Glue to adhere the taped ends to the back of poster board. Pull the tabs under so no tape shows from the front. Place the glued loomwork on a flat surface under a heavy book to dry flat. Now you can add your work to a cuff bracelet, barrette, necklace, or anything you want. Use Tacky Glue and Ultrasuede for the backing. Simple edging works great with loomwork—attach the edging to the Ultrasuede backing and the side warp threads. When you get to the ends, attach the edging to the last row of weaving thread **(figure)**. The sky's the limit, so start soaring!

figure

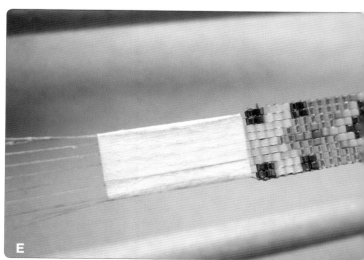

Fringe

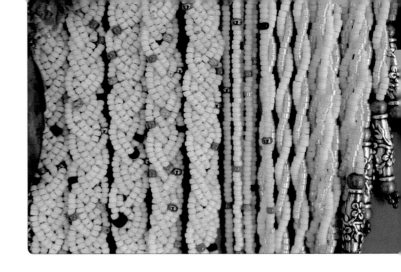

Fringe can really change a simple piece into something more breathtaking. For a long and flowing beaded necklace or earrings, definitely add some fringe. Here, I explain three different kinds of fringe. Twisted Fringe is challenging but worth it. Cascading Fringe uses tube beads and crystals to get a long and full effect. Charming Fringe is an easy way to add larger beads and charms to give your piece a voice. These are just three examples. Let your imagination take you even further.

Twisted Fringe

Twisted fringe has a wonderful fullness and once you get the hang of it, you will love to use it. Use a utility knife to cut a split in one end of a round toothpick. Start as you would any fringe, with the needle exiting the back of your piece. Pick up 25 15º Delicas, a 3mm bead, a 4mm crystal, a cylinder bead, a 4mm crystal, a 3mm, and five 15ºs. Go back up through the 3mm, crystal, cylinder, crystal, and 3mm beads and pick up 25 15º Delicas. Slide the thread into the split toothpick, positioning the toothpick next to the Delicas (leave about ½ in.) **(A)**. Cover the split toothpick and thread with your left thumb and index finger so the thread won't come off **(B)**. With your right hand, start twisting the toothpick. Give it a good 50–75 twists. When the end beads start to buckle, you will know that you have twisted enough. During this process, run your finger down your thread with the needle to release the twist and prevent knots. You want the twist to happen only where the beads are strung. Once you've twisted enough, keep holding the end of the toothpick, and sew in next to where it originally came out on the bottom of your piece **(C)**. Pull the thread all the way through and release the thread from the toothpick. You will need to help get the twisted beads looking as you want. If they aren't twisted enough, you probably didn't twist the toothpick enough or hold the twist enough with your left hand. Be patient here. It may take a few times to get the hang of it. For each new row, add five more Delica beads so the rows get longer as you go. Once you reach the center, begin decreasing by five beads for each row.

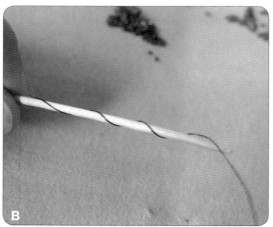

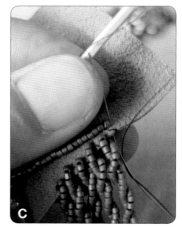

Cascading Fringe

This is very easy fringe and the results are wonderfully full and long. Thread a #12 beading needle with 3 ft. of thread and knot one end. Sew up between the foundation and backing to hide the knot, and exit on the back where you want your fringe to start. For fringe like this **(D)** string: four 9ºs, a tube bead, two 9ºs, a 3mm copper bead, an 8º, a 4mm crystal bead, and five 15ºs. Sew back up through the crystal and the remaining beads in the row; the five 15ºs will form a loop and keep the thread from coming back up. Once you have gone through all the beads, sew through the front of the foundation behind the edging and exit on the backing where you started. Pull the fringe up next to your piece by laying it flat on your work surface. Hold the five 15ºs down on the surface with your left hand and pull the thread up using your right hand; this allows you to pull the strand of beads up closely to your piece and gives you the proper tension. You don't want to pull too hard or the beads will bunch up and not hang nicely. Once the first row is done, sew into the front of the foundation and exit the backing about 1/16–1/8 in. down to start the next row. For the second row string: six 9ºs, a tube bead, two 9ºs, a 3mm copper bead, an 8º, two 4mm crystals, and five 15ºs. Repeat the process as in the first row. Each time you add a new row of beads, add two more 9ºs on the top and an extra crystal to make your strands slowly become longer and fuller. When you get to the middle, simply count back and subtract two 9ºs and a crystal for each remaining strand. Use different beads and quantities to create your own style.

Charming Fringe

Charms add playfulness and fullness to a piece. They can also help establish a theme if you incorporate charms with different meanings. This is just an example using seven rows **(E)**. Start your fringe the same as the Cascading fringe above. The idea is to have different sizes and textures of beads for fullness and different lengths to add depth. You can also add charms along the sides of your piece; this makes the eyes happy. The first row should be short with beads and long with metal feathers or charms. For the second row, add a medium-size cylinder bead with beads on either side. For the third row, add a large, thick bead with another large metal dangle. For the fourth row—the middle and longest row—add another larger cylinder bead and long charm. For the fifth row, keep it long with another long charm, but also attach a shorter charm at the top for fullness: After going back through the row of beads, go back down through three beads, add four small seed beads, a charm, and four more seed beads, and then stitch back up through three beads. For the sixth row, pick up a long cylinder bead and end with a short amount of beads and a long charm. Work the seventh fringe like the first one. For your own look, add different size beads, colors, and charms, and work more rows or fewer. You're the pilot, so let yourself soar.

Animal Totems

When I speak of animals, I include mammals, reptiles, insects, fish, and birds—not just the cute furry ones. All of these creatures are our brothers and sisters, and all that we do to our brothers and sisters we also do to ourselves. When we start to treat our fellow earthlings as we wish to be treated, a magical thing happens: We become one with the earth, at peace. Our world opens up and good things start to happen. Beauty is easier to find. By studying the animals in your area and the ones you have always been attracted to, you can learn and speak a whole new language. It can inspire you in life and your beadwork. For example, you may choose to make a healing and magical piece for you or a loved one— perhaps a necklace in memory of a lost friend that you want to honor. By using different animal totems in your work, you can carry a little bit of their spirit with you. Take the time to reflect upon your life and the animals that have always spoken to you. Choose your own totem and honor your spiritual side. When I have an encounter with animals, I believe it is like medicine. They can bring healing and lessons into your life.

If you talk to the animals they will talk with you and you will know each other. If you do not talk to them you will not know them, and what you do not know you will fear. What one fears one destroys.

— Chief Dan George

In this section, I have included animals I am familiar with. Many of them are my own totems or ones I share my life with in my surroundings. No animal is more important; all are equal. All are beautiful and ugly and unique in some special, wonderful way. The colors and stones I have associated with these animals I have either identified on my own or discovered in my studies and present for you to draw inspiration from. This doesn't mean you can't or shouldn't use colors and stones you desire. I hope you will follow your heart and create your own magical totem piece that carries the oneness of the world.

Hawk

Messenger and Guardian

As the hawk glides overhead, it looks below with a broader vision than we, the grounded souls, can. As humans, we are usually caught up in our thinking heads; hawk teaches us to be observant, to look at things from a broader perspective, and to become conscious. Try to be aware when you come across a hawk—it could be sending you a message from the spirit above, or telling you to soar the skies and reflect on your own life. Hawk is one of my totems, so whenever a hawk appears along my path, I observe what it is doing—hunting, soaring, perching—and then try to apply it to my life at that moment. Hawk has always been my guardian, bringing me light and peace. By incorporating hawk medicine into your work, you can be sure that this guardian will help you be open to signs and help you to make better decisions. You will be more observant and conscious, or perhaps you will open the portal for a message from the spirit world.

Stones: opal and azurite
Colors: red and yellow
Elements: air and fire

Eagle

Spiritual Power and Strength

The eagle soars high to the heavens where the Great Spirit dwells. Eagle lives in the spirit world but also remains grounded on the earth, giving it much balance. Eagle medicine teaches us to gather our courage; we all face challenges and not all of them are easy. We become stronger and more knowledgeable when we learn from our hardships. I was very fearful when I had to start chemotherapy in 2007 for my breast cancer. Not often have I seen an eagle, but weeks before my first treatment, a golden eagle shared the meadow with me as I sat and meditated. It gave me the strength to face my fears and now, years later, I don't regret my cancer, I embrace it. I feel the cancer has taught me so much. A challenge, yes, but a lesson nonetheless. Make a powerful piece by adding eagle for strength and spiritual energy.

Stones: aventurine and agate
Colors: blue and gold
Elements: air and water

Owl

Silent Wisdom

Owl is a bird of magic and darkness; it symbolizes the feminine, the moon, and the night. Are you a night person? I am not, but owl is another one of my totems. I often encounter owl during the daytime and I wear an owl totem necklace every day. Like owl, I prefer being by myself, but I also love and honor my family. Owl can see what others cannot. Use owl's silent observation in a life situation to help you. Owl's wisdom teaches us to pay attention and always speak the truth. Remember to keep silent and go about your business; this may be challenging for some of us. Owl is also associated with fertility and seduction, so be careful when dancing in the moonlight. Some people fear owl, thinking it is an omen of death. Remember, every dark side has a light side, and death is as much a part of life as birth. I like to think of death more as a transformation and an owl encounter has never foreshadowed death for me. Owls always leave me speechless. Use owl in your work to master the magic of silence and the gift of wisdom. Your essence can never be destroyed—only transformed.

Stones: moonstone and angelite
Colors: black and blue
Elements: air and earth

Turtle

Mother Earth

Turtle reminds us to give back to Mother Earth: Walk softly upon her for she is our host and what we do to her, we do to ourselves. Turtle is one of the oldest symbols for planet earth. Those with turtle medicine have longevity and patience. Turtle teaches us the art of grounding, to slow down, and be cautious. Turtle may be slow on its path in life, but it is also very dependable and industrious. Turtle carries its home on its back: The shell is its backbone and ribs. Maybe we, too, could learn from this and carry only what we need. Remember to use your head and knowledge when your life seems upside down. Ground yourself by using some turtle medicine in your piece. Not only will you honor Mother Earth, but you'll honor yourself as well.

Stones: amber and picture jasper
Colors: black and green
Elements: earth and water

Hummingbird

Joy

Hummingbird gets its name from the vibration of its wings as it hovers or flies. Don't forget to hum as you go about life—the vibration can help you heal. Flowers love hummingbirds. Neither could live without the other so a balance is formed. The flowers feed the hummingbirds, bees, and butterflies, who in turn help pollinate the flowers. We are thus reminded to use flowers for healing in our bodies as well as outside them; again, a balance. The feathers of the hummingbird have been used in making love charms and opening the heart. Without an open and loving heart, you will miss all that life has to offer. Unlike any other bird, Hummingbird can fly backward, forward, and sideways, reminding us to be flexible and enjoy what we are doing. The iridescent colors of hummingbird associate it with rain and rainbows. Hummingbirds are also masters of building their homes. I have often watched them as they gather spider webs to use in weaving their nest together. Bring some playfulness, love, joy, and balance to help build your masterpiece.

Stones: quartz and opal
Colors: green and violet
Elements: air and water

Fairywings

Illusion and Transformation

Butterfly: Butterfly teaches us to dance and bring the sweetness back into life. Change is always good. Don't fight it—transformation is part of life, so embrace and enjoy it. Think of the butterfly—what stage of transformation is your life in? The egg stage, larva stage, cocoon stage, or birth? Butterfly helped me through my cancer treatments. I remember being in the cocoon stage for quite a while before I finally took flight once again. Is your masterpiece still in transformation, or ready to be shared with the world?

Dragonfly: It is estimated that dragonflies have been around for more than 180 million years. Once the eggs hatch, dragonflies develop into the nymph stage. It takes up to two years to become a dragonfly. People with dragonfly medicine should examine this two-year cycle and how it may apply to their own lives. Dragonfly has the power of light and anything associated with it will reflect that. Dragonfly can help you to see through the illusion and let your own true gift shine.

Stones: opal and labradorite
Colors: white and blue
Elements: air and water

Hoofed

Stamina, Power, Gentleness, and Prayer

Elk: Whenever I come across elk, I am always reminded to slow down and pace myself. This magnificent animal has the knowledge to know its strength and use it well. By pacing yourself, you can do better and go longer. Use elk medicine to help keep you on track.

Horse: Freedom and power is the medicine horse shares with us. Because of horse, humans are no longer earthbound but free as the wind. Horse reminds us to share and balance our power. True power is looking at the whole journey and sharing pathways with all our brothers and sisters. Compassion, caring, and sharing your gift is the true path to power.

Deer: Follow deer's path into a world of gentleness by accepting people and situations rather than trying to change them. Deer's antlers are symbols of a connection to higher attainment, a reminder to pay attention to one's inner self and perceptions. If you want to make gentle healing and loving peace, incorporate deer medicine.

Buffalo: Buffalo reminds us of the great power of prayer and to be grateful for the abundance we have. Be humble enough to ask and yet grateful for what you receive.

Stones: turquoise and moss agate
Colors: green and black
Elements: earth and air

Canine

Teacher, Trickster, Loyalty, and Flexibility

Wolf: The wolf is very family oriented, yet has its own personal calling. Wolf's path is similar to humans, as we are all part of society and have a carefully defined set of rules, yet we are individuals. Wolf medicine brings the teacher out in us all to help teach and guide the children of the earth. Wolf represents the true meaning of freedom: Is it time to take control of your life or time for a new journey? Let wolf help you know the harmony and discipline of life and still enjoy your freedom.

Coyote: Much like the cartoon character Wile E. Coyote, these animals always seem to get themselves in trouble. This reminds us never to take life and whatever it deals us too seriously. Coyote teaches us to learn from our foolishness. Be on your toes when coyote shows up; I can't count how many times I have laughed at my own seriousness after seeing coyote. Coyotes are also very adaptive, changing where and how they live just to survive. Remember to apply this to your own situation.

Dog: The expression "man's best friend" is no surprise, as that is what dog is. No matter what we do to them, they still love us and are always happy to see us. They will do anything we ask of them and protect us no matter what. Dog teaches us to do for others and to share our gifts and wealth with no questions asked.

Fox: Flexibility and ingenuity are the gifts from fox. Use them to your advantage and let Fox inspire you to navigate life's situations and paths. Be observant and highly adaptable.

Stones: jade and moonstone
Colors: green and brown
Elements: earth and air

Rabbit

Fertility and Fear

Because Rabbit is a common prey animal, nature has blessed it with great fertility. Rabbits produce two to five litters a year—can you imagine? Within 28 days, the young are able to be on their own. This 28-day period is a connection to Rabbit and should be observed if Rabbit is your totem. Rabbit is also associated with fear and reminds us not to be so fearful. Fear may hold you back from challenging situations in your life or moving forward. When I come across Rabbit I watch what Rabbit is doing: Is Rabbit frozen so as not to be seen? If so, I also freeze and apply this to my own life; maybe I need to stop what I am doing and observe and wait. If Rabbit is running, maybe now is a good time to move forward before it's too late. In China, Rabbit is considered good fortune and possesses the powers of the moon. Rabbit moves by hops and leaps and those with a rabbit totem find themselves and their lives doing much the same. Use the teachings of Rabbit in your work to give you confidence to try new things.

Stones: moss agate and onyx
Colors: green and brown
Elements: earth and air

Raven

Magic

Raven and crow are of the same family and size is the only difference between them. There is magic wherever ravens are. They remind us to be aware of the opportunities in life to create and enjoy the magic around us. Raven is the guardian of ceremonial magic and the messenger that carries all energy to its destination. Ravens are one of the most intelligent birds—they can make over 30 different sounds. I love watching them harass my dogs at the compost pile. They retreat just far enough away to be out of reach, but then come back to start the chase all over. The winter solstice is a time of great power for the raven. The sun shines the least on this day, but with each day the light shines a bit more. This time teaches us how to go into the dark and bring out the light. With each trip in, we bring out more light. The more we go into our inner body through mediation or awareness, the more we know about ourselves and our lives. Use the medicine of Raven to make a magical piece that will remind you of the wonders of life and the healing powers brought forth by light and inner peace.

Stones: jasper and onyx
Colors: black and brown
Elements: air and earth

Feline

Power, Secrets, and Independence

Cougar: The medicine of cougar is power. Use it for the good of all, not only thyself. Learning how to balance body, mind, and spirit is part of cougar's gift. If you are a leader, you must be aware of keeping the peace, and always telling the truth. Knowing when to leap is one of cougar's lessons. Are you ready to make a powerful piece?

Bobcat: Bobcat is a solitary animal that enjoys being alone. Bobcat teaches us when to speak, how much to say, and to whom to say it. Be careful, as things can be easily misunderstood. Bobcat also has the gift of knowing secrets and what others may be thinking but doesn't speak or share them. Use this magic of knowing yet being discreet for the better of all.

Cat: Like their larger brothers and sisters, cats are independent. They can be very loving—yet look out when they have other things in mind. Watching them hunt and play is amusing to say the least. My orange tabby cat has no problem feeding himself with mice, while my gray tabby loves bugs and the food bowl. Cats are observant and patient. May we learn the gift of patience and independence from them.

Stones: tigereye and amber
Colors: brown and green
Elements: fire and earth

Bear

Introspection

As winter approaches, bear finds a cave or inviting place to hibernate. I think we all have the same instinct: Toward autumn we want to store some food, bring the wood in, and have some good books on hand. Bear teaches us to spend some time every year entering the safety of our womb. When we meditate with our inner selves, we slow the thinking down; we can now ask questions or reflect on our year. Bear rests in the west: the right side of the brain—our intuitive and female side. Bear awakens in the spring with flowering ideas. Just like her cubs, it may take a few years for those ideas to come into full bloom. Trees are also associated with bear medicine; they are a symbol of fertility and things that grow, and a reminder that we must share our gifts so they can grow and bring beauty into this world. Bring some introspection into life and work by using the medicine of bear.

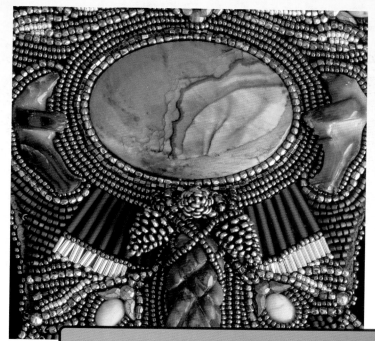

Stones: lapis and amethyst
Colors: purple and blue
Elements: earth and water

Healing Stones and Colors

The stone cabochons available today are amazing. The modern lapidary artist transforms these specimens from the raw form and brings out the true essence of the stone. Healing stones have been around far longer than humans. Like blossoming flowers, these gifts were some of the first in our spiritual existence. We have always been drawn to stones; naturally, we want them near us. They can help heal and cleanse the body and mind, clear out bad energy in a space, or transform your mood. The elements—earth, air, fire, and water—have all helped in the birthing of these gifts. Honor them in the way they were intended. When you incorporate these gifts into your beadwork, you are sharing them with the world and bringing forth the true essence of the universe.

If you ignore beauty,
you will soon find yourself without it...
But if you invest in beauty,
it will remain with you all the days
of your life.

– Frank Lloyd Wright

The colors of beads today are also amazing. There are so many to choose from—far more than a rainbow. Color is all around us—bright, dull, sad, happy—yes, color can speak to us if only we take the time to listen and feel it. We can easily change the mood of our work by simply changing the color or by going from a matte finish to a shiny one. These pages will help you discover and listen to colors, and discern what mood or energy they can bring into your work. By studying stones and colors and incorporating them into our world, we honor them and share their beauty. The world needs their healing gifts and your beautiful work to bring forth positive energy and balance.

White

Purity and New Beginnings

Unlike its opposite, black, white has every color of the rainbow in it. White is a color that goes well with anything; by playing with different shades, such as ivory or beige, you can bring warmth to your work. White is the color of cleanliness and innocence. It makes you feel light and fresh and can bring mental clarity. White works great as a background color. With so many different shades to choose from, you can't go wrong.

Moonstone

As the moon waxes and wanes, Moonstone reminds us of the changes and cycles of life. Moonstone is calming to the emotions and can help relieve the tensions of the day. It can help you to get a restful sleep and is said to eliminate nightmares. Moonstone can help the female reproductive cycle and help alleviate menstrual-related tension.

Quartz

Clear quartz is easily found and is the most common mineral on earth. It is also one of the most powerful and healing stones. Quartz can absorb energy from the sunlight and from nature, and transfer this energy for healing. Using quartz crystals in your work can help other stones transform and stimulate their energy. Quartz can also absorb negative energy in a room or on your body. Placing it back in the sun will clear the negative energy from the stone and cleanse it again. This remarkable stone will bring purity and healing energy into your work.

Black

Resilience and Invisibility

Mysterious black—the color that's absent of color. Black and white represent opposites. While black absorbs and conceals light, white reveals it. Black is linked to the unknown or the unseen. If you want restful emptiness or to be inconspicuous, bring black into your wardrobe. Gray is very similar to black except that it is cooler and more neutral.

Onyx

Onyx is great for giving strength in the face of mental or physical stress. It helps to center you and balance the yin and yang energies in your body. Onyx is said to help with memories of the wearer and thus could help with dementia. Wearing onyx is said to be beneficial to the bones, teeth, and inner ear, and can help absorb sorrow and bad dreams. Let the power of this mysterious stone help ground and steady your life.

Hematite

Hematite, like onyx, can help with memory and give you strength. It can give you confidence and self esteem. Hematite can also help with overcoming addictions and accepting life's mistakes, making them learning experiences. Hematite is known to help with pain: Hold it directly over the pained area or solar plexus chakra (energy center). Next time you have to fly, bring some hematite, as it can lessen the fear of flying and effects of jet lag. This is a beautiful stone with reflective powers; make a special piece for yourself or somebody you know to help with self-healing.

Violet

Inspiration and Spirituality

This awesome color comes from both a strong warm color (red) and a strong cool color (blue). Add more warmth by choosing a shade with more red in it and cool things down by adding blue. Violet is a great color for meditation and for stimulating your imagination. There are many different shades of violet beads and stones available, and just by adding a little splash here and there, you can bring peace and spirituality to your work.

Amethyst

A beautiful stone, amethyst is full of healing energy, and is very easy to find in its raw form or as finished cabochons. Amethyst is powerful, protective, and has a high spiritual vibration. It promotes love and spiritual wisdom, and gives insight into true nature. It is a natural tranquilizer and can block negative energy. Amethyst can be beneficial to the mind: It's calming and helps one focus. It can help relieve physical and emotional pain and is great for the immune system. Not only is amethyst visually appealing, it also benefits our bodies and minds.

Sugilite

This wonderful stone opens and awakens all the chakras in your body. Also known as one of the love stones, it can bring light into some of the darkest moments. Sugilite is great for people working in groups, as it encourages loving communication. Sugilite is also helpful for people with learning disabilities, such as autism and dyslexia, by helping them ground difficulties and overcome conflict with compromise. Cancer sufferers can benefit from sugilite as it can alleviate despair and draw off negative energy.

Green

Growth and Renewal

Green is my favorite color. I love the shades of green in the moss that grows on the forest floor. Green brings forth fertility and growth and is very soothing. Green can bring balance along with a touch of nature into your work. There are so many beautiful green stones in a large variety of shades. Bringing green into your work will also bring peace into your world.

Moss Agate

This is a wonderful stone that sometimes has branching that looks like moss growing in it. Moss agate has a strong connection to nature. People who work with plants can benefit from wearing it; your garden can also benefit if you bury some in the dirt. It is a stone of new beginnings and can release spiritual blockages. Moss agate can help relieve depression, improve self-esteem, and help to develop strength and the ability to get along with others. Moss agate can help speed recovery and help reduce swelling in the lymph nodes as it is anti-inflammatory. By incorporating this stone into your work, you might even attract some money.

Aventurine

Like moss agate, green aventurine is known to bring good fortune and money. Wear it close to your heart, as aventurine also helps with panic attacks and irregular heart rhythms. It's also good for your eyes in case you have been beading too long. Wearing aventurine absorbs electronic smog and protects against environmental pollution. It helps stimulate creativity, giving you belief in your own talents.

Brown

Grounding and Stability

Beautiful, sweet brown…the color of the earth, the ground, the dirt. Brown is a mellow color with many different shades to choose from. This color helps you connect with the earth and bring out the power of your true spirit. It can help keep you grounded and stable. Bring some brown into your work for an organic and wholesome feeling.

Picture Jasper

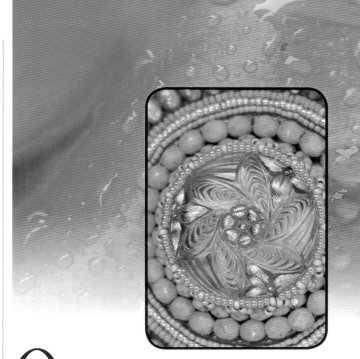

It is said that picture jasper is the Mother Earth speaking to her children, carrying a message from the past for those who can read it. Every stone has a different story to tell. As you look at picture jasper, it looks like mountains and deserts. This stone will help ground you and bring you closer to the earth. Picture jasper is a comforting stone to have around; by incorporating it in your work, you will bring a harmonious feeling with you for your life's journey.

Tigereye

This beautiful stone containing both the energy of the sun and the earth can bring material success. Tigereye can give you strength and courage. It can energize a weak and exhausted person, and create a steady, slow rhythm that will help with decision making and balancing yin and yang. Tigereye can help with your vision, especially at night. Not only is this stone beautiful to look at, but it also carries a healing quality—a balancing of the body and mind.

Orange

Vitality and Endurance

Watch a sunrise or sunset or take a stroll through an autumn forest and you will experience the gift the color orange shares. It is a color to help you understand the mind, body, and spirit; it can also give you ambition and pride in what you do. The color orange is the color of luck and can also bring thoughtfulness and sincerity. If you need change in your life, add some orange; it can help with exploration of new things. Like its sister, red, you don't need a lot to make your point—just a splash will do. Bring some vitality into your masterpiece.

Carnelian

This wonderful stone helps remind you of your unique qualities and strengths. It will help with self doubt and despair. Carnelian can bring positive life choices and encourages success in business and other matters. If you place it near your front door or workplace, it can bring enthusiasm and positivity. Incorporate this amazing stone in your jewelry piece and carry it close to your heart.

Amber

As I walk through the forest near my home, I often see resin dripping from pine trees. It amazes me that this is where amber begins. Amber is tree resin that has solidified and became fossilized. Sometimes you can see tiny insects that have been forever embedded in the stone. This stone is known to absorb negative energy and pain and transform it to positive energy and feelings. It can rebalance the body and help ground you to the earth. Amber is like the sun—its warm, bright energy fills you with peacefulness and wisdom, and helps with depression. Known as the stone of the Mother Goddess, this amazing magical and healing stone should always be nearby.

Blue

Cleansing and Compassion

The color of the skies and the sea is full of depth and stability. Blue is a color of calmness and cleansing. It is a universal color; using it in your bedroom can help you sleep. There are many different blue stones. All of them are both healing and wonderful to gaze upon.

Turquoise

How can anyone resist this amazing stone? There are so many shades and varieties, depending on the mining location. Turquoise is good for detoxifying the body of today's pollutants and negative energy. Place turquoise in your home for protection or your workplace to attract success. Adding some turquoise into a wonderful piece of jewelry can bring you healing and strength, and it has been used for these qualities in amulets throughout history.

Angelite

This stone is associated with angels and thus brings out compassion and kindness. Angelite brings awareness and telepathic communication. It promotes peace and tranquility—something this world needs. Angelite comes from another stone called celestite that has been compressed for millions of years. It's also known as the wiser stone or the Stone of Heaven. It can be tricky to find, but it is worth the look.

Red

Energy and Passion

Red: The color that warms us and gives us energy and passion. Red is associated with the heart and blood. A very stimulating and exciting color, the amount of red used in a piece can determine the level of energy perceived. Red draws attention, so by using red accents you can immediately focus attention on a particular element.

Garnet

Garnet was once worn as a protective talisman. It warned of approaching danger. Today it still offers the same qualities. It also can bring out survival instincts and help in times of need to bring courage and hope. Garnet can help dissolve old patterns of behavior so you will open your heart to new things. Use garnet to stimulate your immune system, improve circulation, and relieve rheumatic joints. This stone is beautiful and it is full of healing energy.

Red Jasper

This beautiful stone has been used for centuries as a protective amulet. It is a sacred stone believed to be the blood of the earth. Red jasper can lift your spirits and keep you focused and energized. It helps with menstrual and menopausal problems. It helps with circulation and warms cold, achy joints. Red jasper offers protection to the wearer from physical and psychic attack and is said to reflect negative energies back to the sender. This stone will calm your nerves and bring you optimal health. Wear this stone close to your skin and feel the passion.

Pink

Acceptance and Peace

This tender and caring color is relaxing to have around. It can diffuse aggressive behavior and bring acceptance and contentment. The quality of the energy in pink is measured by the amount of red it contains. While red and pink represent love—red is hot and passionate, and pink more romantic and compassionate—pink is the sweeter side of red.

Rhodochrosite

This beautiful stone can bring a positive attitude. It represents compassion and selfless love. Rhodochrosite provides great healing. It can bring deep, painful emotions and repressed feelings to the surface, but it also helps you acknowledge and release them. If you're in a new environment, having this stone can bring new friendships and help you feel less lonely. Rhodochrosite can also help increase telepathic communications with a lost loved one or pet. The physical healing energy of this stone can help with asthma, respiratory problems, and migraines.

Rose Quartz

No stone represents love and the heart more than rose quartz. It cleanses and opens the heart at all levels; if you need love in your life, this stone can attract it. Rose quartz can teach unconditional love, compassion, and peace. Physically, rose quartz can help with the heart and circulatory system and can help relieve pain and tension. A beautiful stone to wear and look upon, rose quartz will bring peace into your work and your world.

Metallics

Warmth and Strength

This magical, mystical element can evoke many emotions and feelings. There are different kinds of metal as well as different ways to shape and change it. Incorporating metal beads, shapes, buttons, and findings can make your beadwork stand out and give it value. When you add a metallic edging or fringe, the beadwork becomes framed and finished. Metal has its own essence and when paired with beadwork, a beautiful thing happens.

Gold

The metals in this color family are gold, brass, and bronze. Gold evokes wealth and grandeur, but it also gives warmth and richness. Darker and more mature, brass and bronze give an older feel. Antiquing these metals heightens the sense of age, as if they carry messages from the past. Brightening them brings light and attention.

Copper

This amazing metal is a natural conductor when worn on the body so, if worn with a healing stone, it helps increase healing effects. Copper is known to relieve arthritis and rheumatism. Copper is an attractive metal. Like gold, it brings warmth and comfort. Its reddish hue complements reds and oranges and brings a feeling of energy into any piece.

Silver

Much cooler than gold and copper is the silver color family, including sterling silver, pewter, and white bronze. Silver is sleek and modern and while similar to the color gray, silver is much more exciting. Pewter and white bronze are a bit darker; they have an antique feeling, like a fine head of gray hair suggesting wisdom. Turquoise and blue work well with silver, complementing one another. Pairing silver and gold together is quite fabulous—although they seem opposites, they complement each other.

Cobalt

Intuition and Wisdom

Dark blue is the color of truth, serenity, and harmony. It can help soothe the mind. It is good for cooling, calming, and boosting happiness levels. This beautiful shade of blue can convey importance and confidence, so wear it when you need these attributes. Blue is known to bring peace and is believed to keep the bad spirits away. Cobalt is a bold color, yet when used properly, it can bring the sense of balance and peace.

Azurite

Azurite can help with sleep and understanding your dreams, so use it to seek guidance and communication with your spirit guides. This stone can help bring out leadership qualities and professionalism. It is said to be linked with the lost wisdom of Atlantis. Azurite helps with meditation and channeling, and can urge your spirit to enlightenment. Not only does this stone help with throat, joint, and arthritis issues, it can also help with mental healing and stress relief. Azurite is also found with malachite inclusions—a beautiful mixture of green and blue with the healing qualities of both stones. Use these wonderful stones in your work to help reach deeper insights and intuition.

Lapis Lazuli

Similar to azurite, lapis helps stimulate enlightenment and enhance dream work. This stone can quickly relieve stress and bring a sense of deep inner peace. Lapis can help you find truth and clarity and was known to give insight when worn around the eye. It's not necessary to get the benefits of lapis by only wearing it on your head; place it in your work to mirror the same qualities and benefits of enlightenment and wisdom.

Yellow

Clarity and Communication

Yellow, like a bright sunny day, brings clarity and awareness, warms you, and makes you smile. Especially in the winter months, yellow can lift depression and lethargy. Yellow is a great color to wear if you're a writer or public speaker because it gives you confidence and the ability to express yourself better. Yellow can also help with memory and decision making. If you're tired, nervous, or just need a lift, bring some yellow into your life. Like the sun, yellow will energize you.

Citrine

Known as the sun stone, citrine seems to hold pure sunlight. It is said not to absorb negative energy, but to transform negative energy into positive. This beautiful stone helps with communication and with writing. Citrine will help bring your message forth, whether it's an art project or a conversation with the boss. It's a great stone to have with you all the time as it brings success, wealth, and all good things. Citrine can lift depression, giving you confidence and motivation. A healing stone to help with energizing and recharging, this stone can also help with digestion and constipation. It can also help with balancing hormone problems and may help with hot flashes.

Aragonite

This wonderful stone can help you with patience and being in the moment. Aragonite is a great stone to have during a ceremony, smudging, or rituals honoring the Earth goddess. This environmental stone can help with recycling and conservation. Aragonite is another great stone to help with grounding and deepening one's connection with the earth. The healing properties of aragonite strengthen the immune system, and help with bone and calcium absorption.

The Four Elements

Earth • Fire • Water • Air

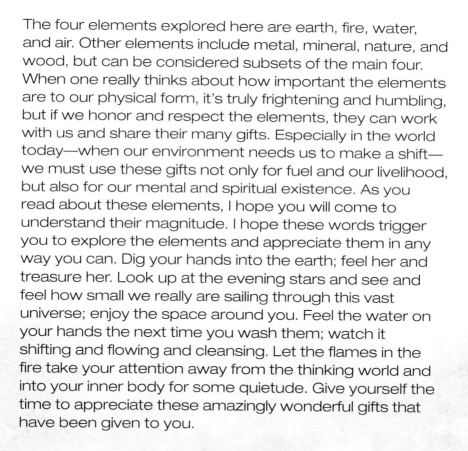

The four elements explored here are earth, fire, water, and air. Other elements include metal, mineral, nature, and wood, but can be considered subsets of the main four. When one really thinks about how important the elements are to our physical form, it's truly frightening and humbling, but if we honor and respect the elements, they can work with us and share their many gifts. Especially in the world today—when our environment needs us to make a shift—we must use these gifts not only for fuel and our livelihood, but also for our mental and spiritual existence. As you read about these elements, I hope you will come to understand their magnitude. I hope these words trigger you to explore the elements and appreciate them in any way you can. Dig your hands into the earth; feel her and treasure her. Look up at the evening stars and see and feel how small we really are sailing through this vast universe; enjoy the space around you. Feel the water on your hands the next time you wash them; watch it shifting and flowing and cleansing. Let the flames in the fire take your attention away from the thinking world and into your inner body for some quietude. Give yourself the time to appreciate these amazingly wonderful gifts that have been given to you.

My soul is the mountains with snow blankets on them.
My soul is an open plain in the desert.
My soul is every living thing!

-Benjamin August Nakai Tarantino (Heidi's son)

Earth

Grounding

The element earth is so comforting and stable: She is the mother that brings forth all life, the flowers in the spring, the beautiful hoofed creatures that graze the open plains, the trees, forest and ground dwellers, along with the insects that live within her. Earth represents body and solidness, home. She is host to us all. Remember to tread lightly upon her, respect her, and love her as she has cared for all living things since her beginning. How would we be able to exist in this physical form without the earth beneath our feet?

People with earth energy are caretakers and grounded builders. They are doers and nurturers. The life force is drawn to people with earth energy because they are calm, organized, and solid. If you have earth energy, your gift is grounding yourself and others. To recharge your earth energy or bring it into your life, spend time in nature and organizing your world.

Animals: hoofed creatures, ground diggers such as chipmunks and groundhogs, insects in the earth, and humans

Stones: jasper, turquoise, azurite, onyx, aventurine, geodes, peridot, tourmaline, and moss agate

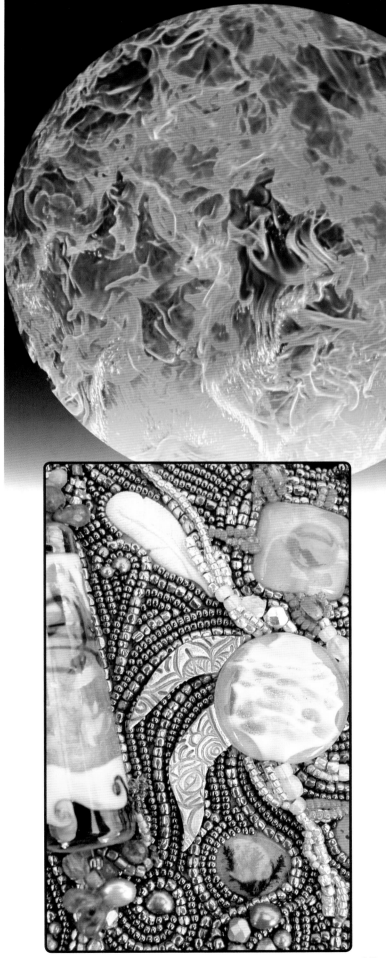

Fire

Energy

The temperature was -30°F this morning. Nothing was stirring; even the birds were still huddled in a hollow tree somewhere, keeping one another warm. Once a fire was lit in the wood stove and we could hear the fire crackling, the whole perception changed: The energy of fire was upon us, filling us with warmth and excitement. Outside the window, Sun was rising, bringing forth the light of day and the glorious light that will awaken the birds and the rest of the world. Our physical form could not exist if not for the warmth and the light of the sun: the greatest source of fire. In photosynthesis, plants absorb the sun's energy and transform it into nourishment. The element fire is essential for our physical bodies as well as our mental well-being. Embrace the sun and be thankful for its gifts. Honor and respect its strength and its destructive abilities.

People with fire energy are usually very spiritual and are aware of their visions and dreams. They are born leaders in serving humanity and compassionate deeds. They are good at helping others find their own true gifts. Fire people need and enjoy having artistic expression; this helps recharge them.

Animals: lions, tigers, cougars, panthers, house cats, snakes, lizards, scorpions, and phoenix

Stones: flint, topaz, garnet, amber, carnelian, tigereye, citrine, hematite, and red jasper

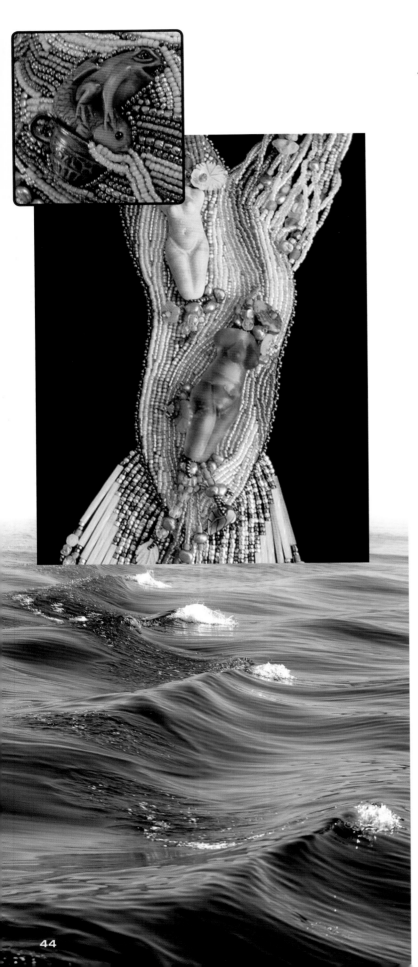

Water

Cleansing

Water is the element associated with emotions and love. Water, like emotions, can be up and down, hard or soft, calming or fierce. We use water everyday to cleanse and nourish our bodies—what a wonderful gift. The clouds in the sky bring forth the rains and snows that purify and satisfy the earth, bringing forth all life. Within the water, more life forms exist—some we have never even seen before, but all are part of the universe and all are equally important. Many creatures flourish in water: otters, whales, frogs, and ducks, to name a few. Cherish the water you consume and wash with; use it sparingly so all creatures may enjoy. Honor water for her calming and soothing beauty and respect her, too, for her strength and power.

Water people have challenges and gifts in the area of emotions and feeling. Others are drawn to water people because they can empathize with their feelings and absorb their emotions. Water is the element of artistic expression and flow. A great way to bring the water element into your life is to be artistic and to be active by walking, swimming, and dancing. By incorporating water into your art and life, a calming and flowing feeling arises, bringing love and peace into this world.

Animals: whales, fish, dolphins, otters, beavers, seals, walrus, sea creatures, water birds, frogs, alligators, and crocodiles

Stones: coral, aquamarine, mother-of-pearl, pearl, lapis, amethyst, sugilite, jade, malachite, and azurite

Air

Breath

What would life be like without sounds, smells, and space? Hearing the birds can remind us to breathe and smile…to be in this moment…listen…it's beautiful. The smell of fresh air swirling by our nose or basil or sage from the garden—all so invigorating yet calming. The sound of music, or better yet, can you hear the silence in between? When you focus on the silence it brings you into mindfulness—a wonderful place to be. Air represents transparent beings—the spirits and fairies. Air is unpredictable and uncatchable. We may be able to use wind to generate power or feel it brush our face, but we are not able to grasp it or see it. Air is the infinity of space, the skies, and that which words cannot describe.

Air people are the communicators. This is their gift; they are conduits and knowers. They are great listeners and because of that they tend to be sounding boards for other people's issues. A way for air people to replenish, or for you to bring the air element into your life, is to bring movement into your body and to bring language into your world by writing or enjoying symbolic art forms. Next time you hear the birds, remember to listen to your breathing, in and out, and spend a moment with life.

Animals: eagles, hummingbirds, hawks, songbirds, and other flying birds; dragonflies, butterflies, bees, ladybugs, and other flying insects

Stones: angelite, azurite, aventurine, mica, and kyanite

Projects

Look at a tree, a flower, a plant. Let your
awareness rest upon it. How still they are, how
deeply rooted in being. Allow nature to teach
you stillness, and fill you with creativeness.
— Eckhart Tolle

The projects in the pages that follow are here to teach you, but also to inspire you and to help you reflect upon your own spirituality and journey in life. I have tried to cover many different ideas, techniques, and designs so you can transform them into your own pieces of jewelry or art forms. May these projects not only challenge you, but also encourage you. As you work your way through the projects, you will master many skills and gain the confidence to design and make your own pieces of art to bring the beauty of the universe into this world for all to enjoy.

Bees
& Trees
earrings

Fertility and Grounding

May we honor the vitality of the bees that move pollen from one flower to the next. Where would we be without them? Trees—wonderful, grounding trees—let's share these gifts. These earrings are an example of what you can make with metal stampings. Go a step further and honor some other life form that you cherish.

Designing

1 Lay out the stampings and cabochons. Play with different stones, colors, and sizes to find the best fit. Choose a color for the foundation, keeping in mind that it should complement the component colors. Find complementary pearls or beads for a simple drop. Would you like a theme or healing energy in these earrings? Now is a good time to plan for that.

Gluing and Stitching

2 Cut a piece of Ultrasuede a bit larger than the components. Keep the top edge straight, so the hole on the top of the stamping can hang over the edge. Leave enough Ultrasuede above the stamping for a row of beads but don't cover the hole.

3 Mix two-part epoxy. Use a toothpick to apply the glue and adhere the stamping to the Ultrasuede. Clean up excess glue with the toothpick. Glue clear cabochons to the foil. Let dry, and then trim excess foil.

4 Using 15º seed beads, start the first row of bead embroidery at the top of the stamping next to the hole **(A)**. Use Backstitch 6 and Backstitch 4 (page 16) to stitch around the stamping, adjusting the number of beads to accommodate the shape of the stamping. After you have made it around, knot the thread on the back and trim the suede.

5 Glue the cabochon below the stamping with epoxy. Clean up excess glue. After the glue has dried, stitch around the cabochon with 15ºs using Backstitch 4. Work another row, starting and ending with a 3mm copper bead.

Trimming and Finishing

6 With a good pair of scissors, carefully trim the piece. Because the earrings are light and small, no lining is needed. With a toothpick and Tacky Glue, glue the beaded stamping to an Ultrasuede backing **(B)** in the same color as the foundation.

7 After the glue is set, trim the excess backing. Begin Simple Edging (page 16) at the point between the stamping and the cabochon. Edge around the whole piece and go back through the first bead. Sew into the backing and exit at the bottom where the dangle will be, exiting the back just to one side of the center.

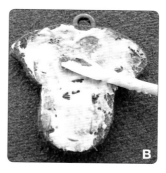

Materials (Bee Earrings)

- 3 grams 15º seed beads, metallic gold
- **2** 8º seed beads, fuchsia
- **2** metal stampings (pulgaNpansas.Etsy.com)
- **2** 6x4mm cabochons
- **2** 4mm pearls
- **6** 3mm copper beads
- Pair of earring wires
- Ultrasuede for foundation and backing
- Two-part epoxy
- Tacky Glue

Tools

- #12 sharp beading needle
- Nymo B
- Toothpicks
- Needlenose pliers
- Scissors

Stitches

- Backstitch 4
- Backstitch 6
- Simple Edging

8 Pick up four 15ºs, a pearl, an 8º seed bead, a 3mm copper, and three 15ºs. Go back through the 3mm, 8º, and pearl. Pick up four 15ºs and sew through the front of the earring bottom in the same spot where the dangle originated. Exit the back, about 3–4mm away from the first group of beads picked up for the dangle. Pick up four 15ºs and go through the dangle beads. Pick up four 15ºs and go through the front and bottom of the earrings where the second leg of the dangles began. Pull all the beads snug. Exit the back of the earring bottom and knot the thread. After knotting, sew in ½ in. **(C)** and cut the thread. Attach the earring wire to the top of the finding.

9 Make a second earring.

Spirit
of the Rings

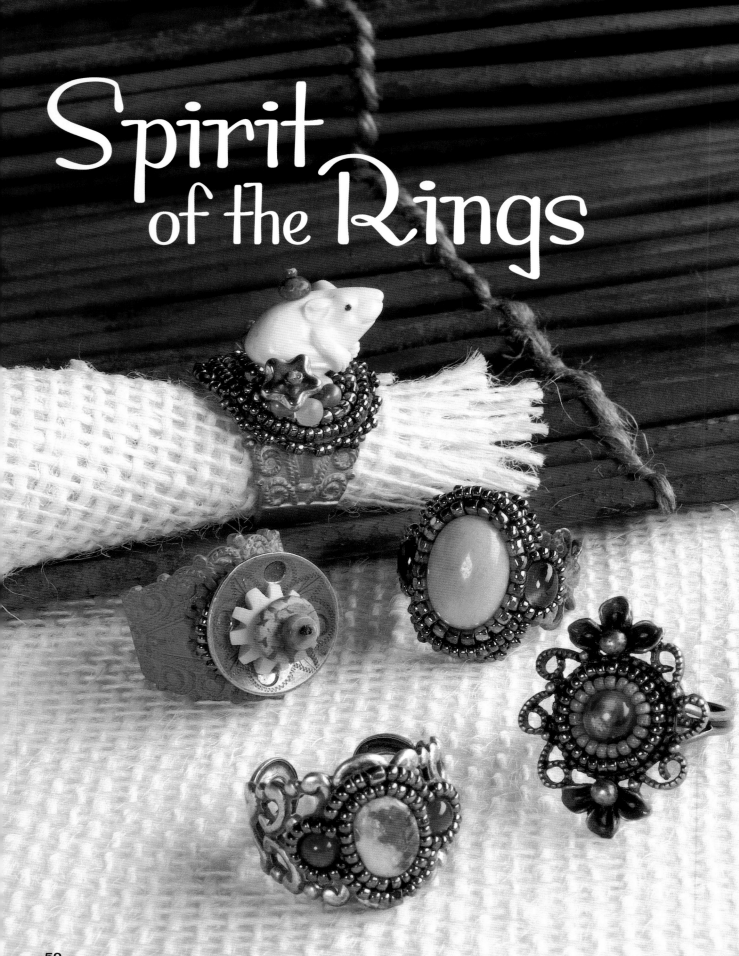

Healing and Compassion

When we hold healing stones close to our skin or in our line of sight, they can remind us to be compassionate and live in the moment. These rings are easy to make. I'll teach you three different approaches. The first, and easiest, uses a simple setting. In the second, you'll attach an embroidered piece to a basic ring shank. The third version is more personal and complex and includes attaching some cool beads to make your special piece.

Materials
- 6mm cabochon
- Ring setting (etsy.com/shop/coolredwell)
- 1 gram 15º seed beads, metallic gold
- 1 gram 15º seed beads, accent color
- Ultrasuede for foundation
- Two-part epoxy

Tools
- #12 sharp beading needles
- Nymo B
- Toothpicks
- Scissors

Stitches
- Backstitch 6

Rings Using a Setting
Designing
1 Pick a stone that's a bit smaller than the setting. You will add one or two rows of 15º seed beads around it. Of course you can use different size beads—have fun here; there are no rules.

Gluing and stitching
2 Using two-part epoxy, adhere the cabochon to a small piece of Ultrasuede. If your cabochon is transparent, glue it to aluminum foil first.

3 Using Backstitch 6 (page 16) and 15º seed beads, add one or two rows of beads. You want the piece to fit into the setting, so the size of the stone and the beads used will determine how many rows you want **(A)**.

4 Trim the beadwork and glue it into the setting with epoxy **(B)**. You're done. Wow, that was easy!

Rings Using a Shank
Designing

1 Select the cabochons you want to use. The larger cabochon used in the picture is 14x7mm and the side cabochons are 4x6 mm. The smaller ring uses a 8x6mm cabochon with 4mm side cabochons. Maybe you have a special cabochon that you have been saving for a special small project. You don't have to use smaller cabochons on the side; you could also use larger beads. If you use a bead, just tack it down and follow the same steps. You may decide to use no side cabochons at all. You're the creator here—be free. If your design is larger than the ring shank, use an Ultrasuede backing and Simple Edging. If your design is smaller than the ring shank, no backing or edging is needed.

Materials
- Center cabochon
- 2 Side cabochons
- Ring shank (etsy.com/shop/dimestoreemporium)
- 50 9º three-cut seed beads, gold iris
- 1 gram 15º seed beads, metallic gold
- Ultrasuede for foundation and backing
- Two-part epoxy

Tools
- #12 sharp beading needle
- Nymo B
- Toothpicks
- Ruler
- Fine-tip marker
- Scissors

Stitches
- Backstitch 6
- Backstitch 4
- Simple Edging

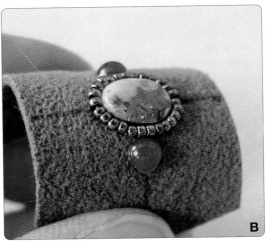

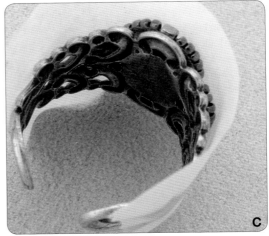

Gluing and Stitching

2 Rings are a great place to use up small pieces of Ultrasuede. If you are adding side cabochons or beads, mark center lines with a fine-tip marker. Glue the center stone to the Ultrasuede. Glue any clear cabochons to aluminum foil **(A)**.

3 Stitch the first row of beads using Backstitch 6 and the beads of your choice.

4 Glue the side stones to the Ultrasuede, and while the glue is still wet, hold the piece onto the ring shank **(B)**. You may need to move the side stones closer to the first row of beads.

5 After the glue has dried, stitch around the side stones using Backstitch 4 (page 16) and 15º metallic gold seed beads. You may want to add a second row of beads around the larger cabochon.

6 Trim the excess Ultrasuede. If you're making the smaller ring that does not extend beyond the ring shank, glue it to the top of your ring shank. Use a piece of masking tape to help anchor it in place **(C)**.

Repeat to finish the larger ring, but before gluing the ring to the shank, cut a piece of Ultrasuede for backing that's the same size as the beaded center stone, but not including the side stones. Glue on the backing, allow the glue to set for 10 min., and trim any excess Ultrasuede.

Tip Use Tacky Glue instead of epoxy, if you wish, because the edging will add extra security.

7 Begin Simple Edging (page 16) in a corner where the two rows of 15º seed beads meet.

8 Continue Simple Edging around the piece. When you get to the end, rather than edging around the small side stone, slip your needle back through the last three beads in Simple Edging and down through the fourth bead. Sew through the foundation and to the other side of the shank. The needle should exit the same place you started on the opposite side **(D)**.

After you finish edging, you have a sweet ring to help bring you to mindfulness.

Rings Using Your Imagination

Designing

1 Finding just the right bead is half the fun. For one ring, I found this way-cool mouse bead made from fossilized walrus tusk. For the other ring, I drilled a hole in a button. These instructions describe both rings.

Place the item you're thinking of using on your finger. How does it look? Is it too big or just right? The sky is the limit here. Be creative. Try something you think would never work. Oddly enough that's what happened with Miss Mousey. I placed her on my finger and asked, "Why not?"

Gluing and Stitching

2 Miss Mouse ring: Glue the mouse bead to a small piece of Ultrasuede. After the glue has dried, use the center hole of the bead to add some other beads and to help anchor the bead in place **(A)**. If your hole got filled with glue, use a drill to clean it out. Using Backstitch 6 (page 16), put a few rows of beads around your centerpiece. I wanted to have what looked like flowers coming out of the ground, so I tacked down some dagger beads and a flower bead.

3 After you're done, trim the piece and add Simple Edging (page 16). After the piece is glued to the ring shank it will be harder to edge, so now is a good time.

4 Glue your masterpiece to the ring shank **(B)**. If the shank has holes in it, you may need to clean the inside with alcohol.

5 Stacked ring: I liked the idea of stacking beads and using an old button for this ring. If your button is without a hole, drill one. Stack disk beads on top to see how it will look. My button was curved and hard to bead around, so I glued it to a small disk bead with Tacky Glue. I didn't want the bead to be permanent—just to be used as a guide—so I stitched two rows of 15ºs around the turquoise and then removed it **(C)**. The button rests in this circle nicely. Glue the metal button in the circle. After the glue has dried, sew on the stacked beads **(D)**. If the hole got filled with glue, drill it open.

A

B

Materials

- Bead or button
- Ring shank (etsy.com/shop/ charmsgalore
- 15º seed beads: 1 gram each of metallic gold, green, red
- Accent beads
- Ultrasuede for foundation
- Two-part epoxy

Tools

- #12 sharp beading needles
- Nymo B
- Toothpicks
- Scissors
- Drill (optional)

Stitches

- Backstitch 6
- Tacking
- Simple Edging

6 Trim the piece and add Simple Edging. Glue the piece to the ring shank. You may need a toothpick to help flatten the foundation to the ring. Be patient here and keep working it.

7 After the glue has dried, thread a #12 sharp needle on a length of beading thread and knot one end. If your ring shank has a hole in the back, sew into the hole and exit on top next to the rows of beading. String several inches of 15ºs

in red and green, and wrap them around the bottom of the metal disk going back through beads a few times for strength **(E)**. This helped make the disk look better from underneath and make the finished piece stronger.

8 After you have sewn through the strand of beads, tie a few knots **(F)**, exit the row of beads, and cut the thread.

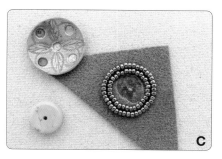

C

D

E

F

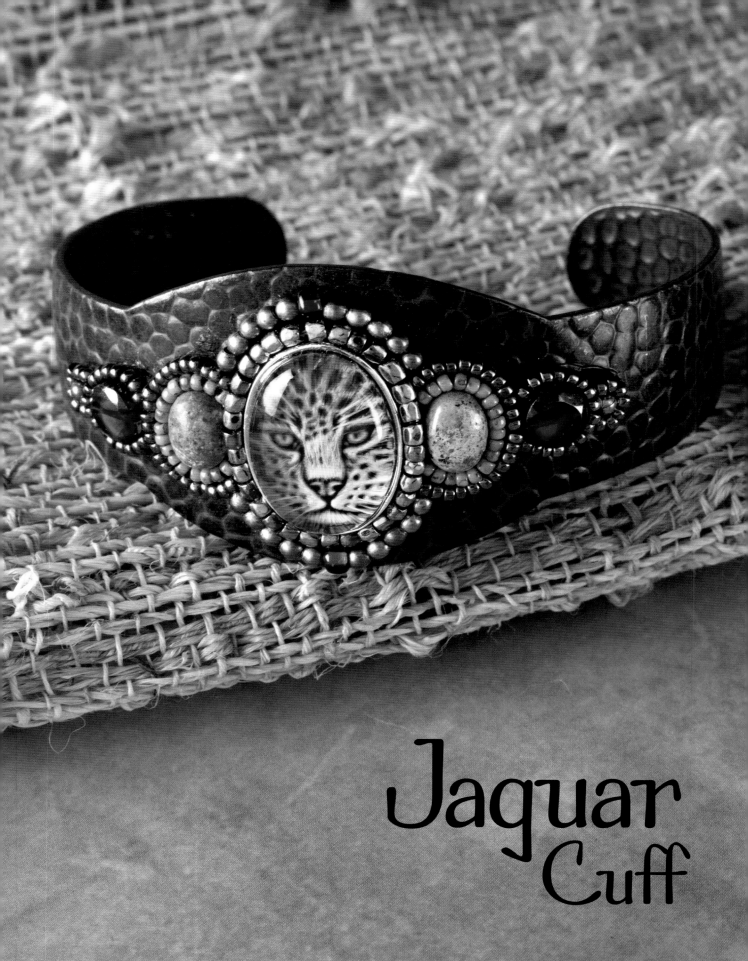

Jaquar Cuff

Energy and balance

The combination of amber, garnet, and feline is perfect for energy. Turquoise cleanses the energy, making this a healing and protective talisman. This bracelet is so easy to make and you can use any cuff you have available. I love the texture and color of this one from Designer's Findings.

Designing

1 If you don't have an amber jaguar, use another stone or just a plain amber stone. The color cuff you use should help you decide the color of the Ultrasuede; pick a color that matches the cuff, so you won't even notice it. You can use a permanent marker that matches the cuff to color the edges of the Ultrasuede after it is trimmed.

Gluing and Stitching

2 Cut a piece of Ultrasuede 3x1½ in. and mark the center lines using a ruler and marker. Glue the amber cabochon in the middle with epoxy, using the lines as a reference.

3 After the glue has set, stitch a row of 9° three-cut beads around the cabochon using Backstitch 6 (page 16).

4 Glue the turquoise cabochons next to the row of 9° three-cut beads. Use the marked lines to help with placement. After they are glued and the glue is still wet, place the Ultrasuede on the curve of the cuff. You may find that they need to be pushed a bit closer to the 9°s **(A)**. Anytime you curve something flat, you may find a gap.

5 After the glue has dried, stitch a row of 15° turquoise beads around the cabochon using Backstitch 6. Sew in the corner next to the cabochon and the 9°s. Next, stitch a row of 15° metallic seed beads next to the turquoise beads using Backstitch 6.

6 If these are clear cabochons, glue them to aluminum foil so the true essence of the stone shines through. Glue the garnet cabochons in place, using the marked lines for placement **(B)**.

7 When the glue has dried, stitch a row of 15° metallic gold seed beads around the garnet cabochons using Backstitch 6. After stitching around the first garnet, stitch a 2mm copper bead next to it. Go through the bead a few times for security. Using Backstitch 4, stitch a row of 15°s around the 2mm bead.

Materials

- 30x20mm amber jaguar cabochon (Rio Grande)
- **2** 6xmm turquoise cabochons
- **2** 6mm garnet cabochons
- **22** 2mm copper beads
- **2** 8° seed beads, accent color
- **50** 9° three-cut seed beads, gold iris
- 2 grams 15° seed beads, metallic gold
- 1 gram 15° seed beads, turquoise
- Bracelet cuff (Designers Findings)
- Ultrasuede for foundation
- Two-part epoxy

Tools

- #12 sharp beading needle
- Nymo B
- Toothpicks
- Scissors
- Fine-tip marker
- Ruler

Stitches

- Backstitch 6
- Backstitch 4

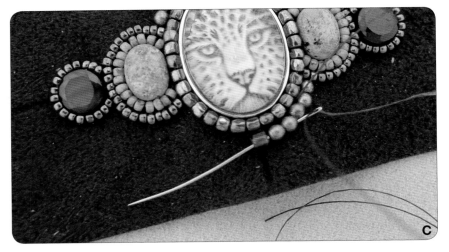

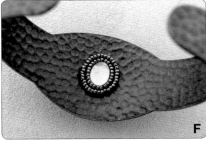

8 Repeat on the opposite side of the design. Knot the thread to get to the other side or go through the already beaded rows (this will also reinforce your piece).

9 To add some accent beads above and below the focal cabochon, sew through the piece to exit in the corner between the last row around the turquoise cabochon and the 9ºs. Using Backstitch 6, surround one edge of the amber cabochon with five 2mm copper beads, an 8º accent bead **(C)**, and five 2mms. This may vary, depending on the size cabochon you used and also the size beads you used. As with every row, go back through for reinforcement and to make the beads line up nicely. Add a matching row of beads along the remaining edge of the amber cabochon.

Trimming and Finishing
10 Trim your masterpiece **(D)**.

11 Glue the piece to the center of your cuff using epoxy **(E)**. Use isopropyl alcohol to clean up any excess glue, and carefully and firmly press the piece in place.

12 If you want to add some extra healing power, glue a cabochon of your choice to some scrap Ultrasuede and add a few rows of 15º beads using Backstitch 4 or 6. Trim. Glue it onto the back of your cuff **(F)**.

Flower Fresh
Earrings

Reflecting Your True Essence

Spiritual teacher Thich Nhat Hanh says our hands and eyes are like flowers, and when we smile we blossom. Meditate and say "flower" to yourself as you inhale and "fresh" as you exhale. I do this throughout my day to remember to be like a flower—fresh and showing my true essence. I love old buttons, but be creative and use anything you may already have in your stash.

Designing

1 Replace the button with a cabochon or a metal stamping. Or, use a cabochon instead of the briolette. Omit the fringe or shorten it. Change the bead colors.

Gluing and Stitching

2 Use wire cutters to cut the button shanks. With epoxy, glue the buttons to the Ultrasuede, leaving room around them **(A)**.

3 Using Backstitch 6 (page 16), stitch a row of 15º seed beads around the buttons.

4 Glue a clear briolette or cabochon to foil **(B)**. After the glue has dried, trim the foil and glue the briolettes below the 15ºs **(C)**.

5 After the glue dries, tack the briolettes down. Stitch a row of 9º gold iris around the briolettes with Backstitch 4 **(D)**.

6 Stitch 8º accent beads on either side of the briolettes. Go through the 8ºs a few times to secure **(E)**. Using Backstitch 4, add a row of 15ºs around the 8ºs.

7 For the final row, exit in the corner between the 15ºs surrounding the 8º and the button. Add a row of 9ºs around the button using Backstitch 6.

8 Trim the backings of your beautiful earrings **(F)**.

Materials

- **2** vintage flower buttons
- **2** 4x6mm amethyst briolettes (Fire Mountain Gems and Beads)
- **14** dagger beads
- **14** 4mm Czech beads, dark purple
- **10** 4mm Czech beads, light purple
- **6** 4mm Czech beads, metallic gold
- **2** 4mm Czech beads, light gold
- **14** 3mm copper beads
- **18** 8º seed bead, opal
- **14** 12mm bugle beads
- 1 gram 9º three-cut seed beads, gold iris
- 3 grams 15º seed beads, metallic gold
- Pair post earrings with backs
- Ultrasuede for foundation and backing
- Two-part epoxy
- Tacky Glue
- Poster board

Tools

- #12 sharp beading needle
- #12 beading needle
- Nymo B
- Toothpicks
- Scissors
- Fine-tip marker

Stitches

- Backstitch 4
- Backstitch 6
- Simple Edging

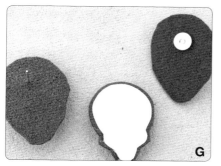

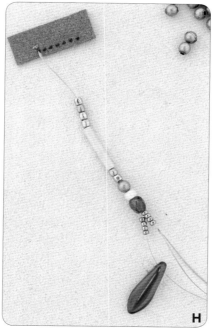

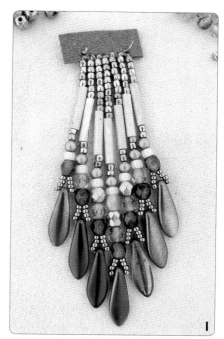

Finishing and Fringe

9 Trace around the earrings on poster board. Trim ⅛ in. smaller than the earrings. Adhere the lining to the backs of the earrings with Tacky Glue and press firmly in place.

10 Lay the earrings on the Ultrasuede and cut the backing a bit bigger than the earrings. You will trim it once it's glued.

11 Mark the location of the earring post on the reverse side of the Ultrasuede. Use a hole reamer or a large needle to punch a hole and push the earring post through.

12 Glue the backing (with epoxy) to the back of the beaded earring **(G)**. Spread a small amount of glue around the post back to help set it in place. After the glue sets, trim the excess Ultrasuede.

13 Cut a ¼x¾-in. piece of Ultrasuede to anchor the fringe. Mark seven dots along the center of one edge, placing them ¹⁄₁₆ in. apart. Thread a #12 beading needle on 1 yd. of thread, and knot. Sew through the first dot on the left and go back through next to the dot to hide and secure the knot.

14 Stitch the fringe:
Row 1: Pick up four 9° gold iris, a bugle, two 9°s, a 3mm copper, an 8°, a 4mm

dark purple, four 15° metallic golds, a dagger, and four 15°s. Go back through the 4mm dark purple and the rest of the beads. Sew through the front of the Ultrasuede at the first dot **(H)**. Pull the row snug (but not too tight). Sew through the next dot.
Rows 2–4: Repeat Row 1, adding two more 9°s to start and a new 4mm before the 4mm dark purple each time.
Rows 5–7: Repeat Rows 2–4, decreasing by two 9°s and one 4mm each time.

15 Knot on the back next to the last row and cut the thread **(I)**.

16 Glue the fringe to the back of the trimmed earrings with Tacky Glue **(J)**. After the glue is set, trim the excess Ultrasuede from the fringe.

17 Start Simple Edging (page 16), next to the 8° where the fringe Ultrasuede is attached. Sew from the back of the foundation and through the front to hide the knot **(K)**. Continue Simple Edging using 15° metallic gold seed beads.

18 Finish the second earring. Wear your earrings and smile like a fresh flower.

Owl cuff

Wisdom and Silence

Wearing this piece makes one fee' wisdom and silence of owl medicine will transfer to the wea. turquoise bring healing and protection, but you can replace them whatever energy you wish. Laura Mears truly captures the essence of c wonderful porcelain piece.

A

Materials
- Laura Mears sitting owl
- 6mm amethyst cabochon
- 6x4mm turquoise cabochon
- 1¼ in. brass cuff
- **200** 9º three-cut seed beads, gold iris
- **20** 11º hex-cut Delicas, metallic silver
- **20** 11º Delicas, metallic gold
- **34** 12mm bugle beads
- 5 grams 15º seed beads, metallic gold
- Black Ultrasuede for backing
- Tan Ultrasuede for foundation
- Poster board
- Two-part epoxy
- Tacky Glue

Tools
- #12 sharp beading needles
- Nymo B
- Toothpicks
- Ruler
- Fine-tip marker
- Scissors
- Sandpaper (coarse 60 grit)

Stitches
- Backstitch 4
- Backstitch 6
- Simple Edging

Designing

1 Change the colors of the bugle beads along with the stones to get a totally different feel. You can also use another oval centerpiece in place of the owl.

2 I used black Ultrasuede for the backing, as it gives the piece such a striking look. I used tan Ultrasuede for the foundation only so I could mark the placement of the bugle beads. Cut a 4x3-in. piece of light-colored Ultrasuede. Using a ruler, mark center lines.

Gluing and Stitching

3 With sandpaper, rough up the back of the owl and the cabochons you will be using to ensure a good bond with the glue. Using two-part epoxy, center and glue the owl to the Ultrasuede **(A)**. Glue a clear cabochon, such as the amethyst, to a piece of aluminum foil. Let dry, and then trim away any excess foil.

4 After the glue has dried, stitch the first row of beads around the owl with Backstitch 6 (page 16) using 9º Czech three-cut gold iris beads.

5 Use epoxy to glue the amethyst above the owl and the turquoise below the owl. Snug the cabochons against the beads and line them up with the center line.

6 After the glue has dried, stitch a row of beads around the amethyst with Backstitch 6 and 15º metallic gold seed beads. Stitch a second row of beads with metallic silver Delicas. Knot the thread and trim the ends. Stitch a row around the turquoise cabochon with Backstitch 6 and metallic gold Delicas. Stitch a second row of metallic gold 15ºs.

7 Add a row of beads next to the first row of 9º three-cuts, starting next to the 15ºs, surrounding the turquoise cabochon. Using Backstitch 6 and the metallic gold 15ºs stitch a row all the way up to the metallic silver Delicas. After the row is complete, go back down through the row to reinforce it. Start another row next to it using 9º three-cuts. Repeat on the

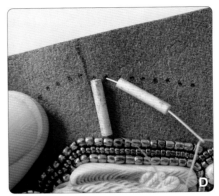

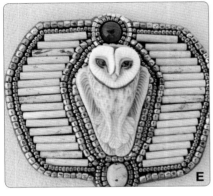

opposite side of the owl **(B)**. Always go back through the rows of beads—this makes them stronger and puts any loose beads in order.

8 Place 17 bugle beads on one side of the beaded owl. Using a toothpick and the center line as a guide, align the bugle beads. Place one bead on the center line and eight on each side. After the beads are lined up as you wish, use a fine-tip marker and put a dot at the end of each bead to guide you as you begin to sew **(C)**.

9 Thread a #12 sharp beading needle and knot the thread. Position the center bugle bead on the line and sew up next to the row of 9º three-cut beads where the end of the bugle rests. Pick up the bugle and come back through the Ultrasuede at the dot. Repeat **(D)** until all the bugle beads are in place. Go back through each bugle bead to strengthen and fix any that are not lying correctly. Repeat on the opposite side of the owl.

10 Stitch a row of 15º metallic golds and then a row of 9º three-cuts around the bugle beads using Backstitch 6. If there is any space between the top and bottom bugle beads where they meet the inside row of the three-cuts, add one or two 15ºs as needed.

Trimming and Finishing

11 Trim your sweet beaded owl, being careful not to cut any threads **(E)**.

12 If you're using black Ultrasuede as the backing and siding, use a black permanent marker to color the excess tan Ultrasuede so it will blend into the backing and not be noticeable **(F)**.

13 Cut a 6½x1⅜-in. piece of poster board for a pattern. Mark a line at 6⅛ in. (the inside dimension of the cuff). Mark the center.

14 Trace the pattern onto the backing Ultrasuede. If you're using black Ultrasuede, it is a bit hard to mark a line. Try different pens until you get one that makes a visible mark. Save this for gluing on top of the cuff.

15 Trace the pattern onto the black Ultrasuede, leaving enough space along the edges to accommodate the height of the owl centerpiece. Mark the center of the traced pattern and rest the owl centerpiece on the Ultrasuede. Trace around the owl **(G)**. Cut out the centerpiece, including the straight sides and the center portion that will go behind the owl. It's important to keep the lines straight because once you glue the Ultrasuede to the cuff, it's harder to trim along the sides.

16 Using Tacky Glue **(H)**, adhere the Ultrasuede to the inside of the cuff and trim the ends **(I)**. As I mentioned before, if you cut the lines straight you should not need to trim the sides.

17 Glue the longer piece of Ultrasuede to the top of the cuff using Tacky Glue **(J)**. After the glue has set, trim the ends of the cuff using the pre-trimmed Ultrasuede as a guide.

18 Place the beaded owl on a piece of poster board and trace around him. Cut the poster board ⅛ in. smaller than the tracing. This is the lining for your owl—

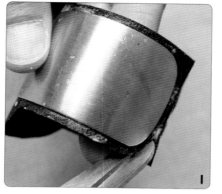

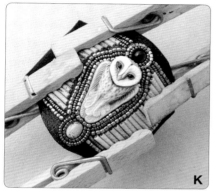

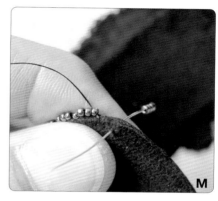

make sure it is cut smaller or you will have to sew through poster board and you will have sore fingers!

19 After the poster-board lining is cut to size, attach it with Tacky Glue to the back of the beaded owl. Next, glue the owl to the top of the cuff. Use Tacky Glue and make sure that the glue gets spread evenly and close to the ends where it will rest on the cuff. Clamp the centerpiece to the cuff **(K)** and clean up any excess glue with a cotton swab and water. I like to use clothespins as clamps.

20 After the glue has set, trim the excess Ultrasuede above and below the beaded owl **(L)**.

21 Now you're ready for edging. If you have black Ultrasuede, use black thread. If you don't have black thread, you can always use a permanent marker to hide any stitches.

22 Thread a #12 sharp beading needle and knot the thread. Start Simple Edging (page 16) using 15º metallic gold seed beads in a corner. Sew between the

backing and the foundation so the needle comes out of the front of the foundation and the knot is hidden. Pick up four 15ºs and continue Simple Edging all around the piece **(M)**. When you come back to the beginning, you may need to adjust the number of beads for the final stitch. Direct the needle down through the top of the bead you started with and out through the back of the backing **(N)**.

23 Tie a knot against the Ultrasuede. Sew down next to the knot and out about ½ in. away. Pull the thread and cut. You now have the most wonderful owl cuff ever—how cool is that?

Butterfly Barrette

Transformation and New Beginnings

Butterfly represents transformation. The vibrant colors in this piece bring clarity and endurance, but you can change them to create whatever your world needs. If you don't wear barrettes, you can easily make this into a cuff bracelet or necklace.

Designing

1 Use the pattern (page 66) to get started. Play with different colors to customize your butterfly. Just changing the background color can evoke a different feeling. Change the color or size of the stones, or maybe use no stone at all—make this your own special design. Modify the fringe if you wish. You may not find the exact color of metal drops, but you may have something else in your bead stash. Omit the fringe for a more practical everyday barrette.

Looming

2 Warp the loom (page 20). The pattern included is for 25 beads across, so you will need 26 warp threads. Tie 1 yd. of Nymo on the left warp thread if you're right-handed or on the right warp thread if you're left-handed.

Note: This barrette is 50 rows long but the pattern is only 25 rows. Work the pattern as shown, starting with the bottom row, and then repeat the pattern in reverse to form the other butterfly half.

3 As always with loomwork, the first row is the trickiest. Pass the beads under the warp threads and sew back through the beads, keeping the needle on the top of the warps. I find that after the second row is on, it's easier to pull the two rows snug. Don't over tighten—just get the beads snug enough that the Delicas rest peacefully next to each other.

Note: To end a thread, tie it off on the left end warp thread, and hide the remaining thread by going through one of the rows of beads and cutting it. Add a new thread by tying on to the left warp thread and continuing. You can hide the tail by pulling it through a row or tacking it along with the end warp thread.

4 After the loomwork is done, use clear fingernail polish to coat the ends of the warp threads and the knots. This helps secure the loomwork ends once the piece is taped and cut. With the fingernail polish still a bit tacky, use masking tape to tape the ends. Tape the warp threads so they are in bit narrower then the loomwork— this way you won't see the tape once it's folded over.

5 Cut the taped ends a bit smaller and smooth the tape flat using a small ruler or flat object. This helps keep the tape holding the warp threads tight. Cut a small piece of interfacing slightly smaller than the loomwork and, using Tacky Glue, adhere it to the back of the loomwork (which can be either side) **(A)**.

Materials

- **1–4** grams each Delica listed on pattern
- **50** 11º Delicas for edging, AB olive
- **50** 15º seed beads, metallic gold
- **50** 15º seed beads, black
- **16** 8º seed beads, fuchsia
- **8** metal patina dangles (Fire Mountain Gems and Beads)
- **2** 20x7mm feather patina dangles (Fire Mountain Gems and Beads)
- **2** 6x4mm cabochons
- **8** 4mm Czech fire-polished beads, gold
- **6** 4mm Czech fire-polished beads, metallic gold
- **6** 4mm Czech fire-polished beads, matte black
- **16** 3mm copper beads
- **16** 2mm copper beads
- 3¼ in. French-style barrette with removable clasp
- Ultrasuede
- Two-part epoxy
- Tacky Glue
- Poster board
- Fabric interfacing

Tools

- #12 sharp beading needles for edging and stone
- #12 beading needles for weaving and fringe
- Nymo B
- Loom
- Toothpicks
- Clear fingernail polish
- Masking tape
- Fine-tip marker
- Utility knife
- Scissors

Stitches

- Loomwork
- Simple Edging
- Fringe

A

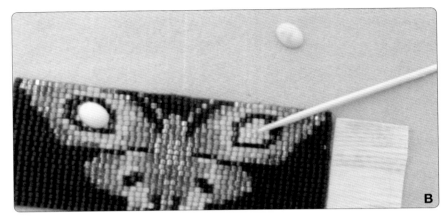

B

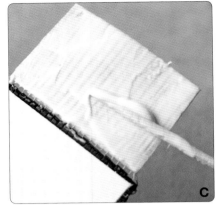

C

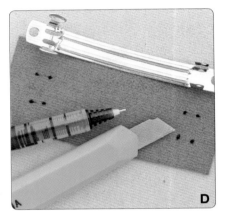

D

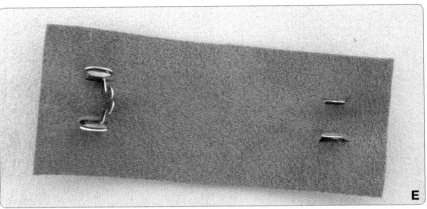

E

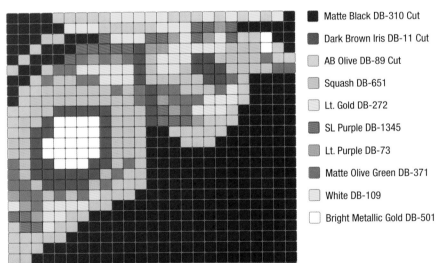

■	Matte Black DB-310 Cut
■	Dark Brown Iris DB-11 Cut
□	AB Olive DB-89 Cut
▨	Squash DB-651
□	Lt. Gold DB-272
▨	SL Purple DB-1345
▨	Lt. Purple DB-73
▨	Matte Olive Green DB-371
□	White DB-109
□	Bright Metallic Gold DB-501

Finishing and Fringe

8 Cut a piece of poster board a bit smaller than the loomwork. Using Tacky Glue, adhere it to the loomwork and interfacing. Glue the end tabs, folding them over so they rest on the back **(C)**.

9 Cut a piece of Ultrasuede close to the same size as the loomwork (trim any excess once it's glued). Remove the clasp part of the barrette and place the barrette on the Ultrasuede. Mark where the pieces of metal hinge will push through the Ultrasuede. Using a utility knife, cut slits **(D)**. Test the barrette by pushing it through the slits—you may need to adjust the cut. After you have a good fit, glue the barrette to the Ultrasuede. It's easier to put the Tacky Glue on the back of the barrette than to slip the Ultrasuede onto the barrette **(E)**.

10 After the Ultrasuede is glued, glue the loomwork to the top of the barrette using Tacky Glue. Make sure to glue it upright. If you're left-handed, the hinge should be toward the front of the head. Hold the

6 After the Tacky Glue has set, use two-part epoxy and a toothpick to glue the cabochons for the circle, or eyes, of the wings **(B)**. Put a dab of glue on the loomwork and the backs of the stones. Clean up any excess with the toothpick.

7 After the epoxy has dried, add a row of 15° black beads around the cabochon:

Thread a 2-ft. length of thread with a #12 sharp needle and knot the end. Sew up through the back of the loomwork and interfacing next to the cabochon. Using Backstitch 6, bead around the stone. After you are done, sew back through the loomwork and knot on the back of the interfacing. The interfacing acts as a foundation to hold the knots and stitches.

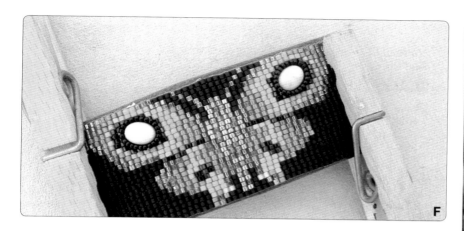

F

loomwork to the barrette with clothespins until the glue dries **(F)**.

11 Trim any Ultrasuede that extends beyond the loomwork; the Ultrasuede should be even with the loomwork.

12 Trim with Simple Edging (page 16). Thread a #12 sharp needle with a 3-ft. length of thread and knot the end. Sew down through the Ultrasuede on the inside close to the middle of the barrette at the starting point for one end of the fringe to hide the knot. Sew between the two edge warp threads and pull taut. Pick up four Delica edging beads. Skip two rows of beads, and sew through the back of the Ultrasuede between the two edge warp threads and between the two beads **(G)**. Pull taut. Sew back up through the last bead and pick up three Delicas. Repeat to complete the edging. When you reach the ends of the loomwork you won't have a warp thread to sew under, so instead, sew under the thread from the last row of beads. Repeat along the ends, skipping three beads each time. Edge around the barrette until you have one edging stitch remaining. For the final stitch, pick up this bead (depending upon the spacing, the amount of beads may vary) and sew down through the top of the first bead that the edging started with. Sew through the Ultrasuede exiting the back of the barrette.

13 If you're not planning to add fringe, tie a knot on the back of the Ultrasuede. Sew down next to the knot and down about ½ in. Pull the thread tight and cut. If you are adding fringe continue to step 14.

14 Sew into the loomwork and exit one of the center rows with the needle going in the direction the fringe will be added. This will help determine where to place the fringe: Flip the piece over, and, with a fine-tip marker, put a faint dot at the middle (where the thread is exiting). The fringe will be spaced every ⅛ in. If you want one long middle fringe, mark an equal number of dots to the left and right of the center. I have two strands in the middle and three dots on either side of the center (eight dots total for eight strands).

15 Sew through the piece so the needle comes out of the Ultrasuede at the dot furthest to the left. I like using a #12 beading needle for fringe. Change the needle at this point if you haven't already. Pick up three 15º metallic gold seed beads, a 2mm copper bead, a feather dangle, a 2mm, and three 15ºs. Pull the beads down next to the Ultrasuede, and push the needle through the front of the piece just opposite the dot. The needle should not go through the actual loomwork, but rather, next to the warp thread and over the edging and exit again through the same dot on the back. The rest of the fringe will be attached to the Ultrasuede on the back—only the two end feathers loop around the front.

16 For the second fringe, sew through the Ultrasuede to exit the next dot. Add a 3mm copper bead, an 8º fuchsia bead, a 4mm metallic gold, an 8º fuchsia, a 3mm copper, three 15º metallic golds, a 2mm copper, a patina dangle, a 2mm copper, and three 15ºs. Sew back up through the last 3mm and the rest of the beads on the

G

H

strand. Sew back through the Ultrasuede at the dot and exit the next dot. Pull the beads snug. Work the third fringe the same way as the second, but add a 4mm Czech bead. Continue adding a 4mm Czech bead for each fringe you make until you reach the center. Then, decrease one 4mm Czech bead for each fringe. After you have completed the fringe, end it as in step 12 **(H)**.

17 Replace the removable clasp.

Peace
Necklace

Peaceful Inspiration

The calming colors in this loomed necklace bring peace and inspirational essence. Change the colors to bring whatever energy you want. Add special charms to make your own statement. This looks like a complicated piece, but is really quite easy.

Designing

1 Use the pattern (page 71) to get started. Change the colors to make a necklace that reflects whatever mood you want. Choose different charms and larger beads that complement the loomwork. You don't have to go buy these items; chances are you already have them in your stash. If you'd rather use another pattern, that's fine. Make it larger or smaller, if you'd like. I find needlepoint patterns work well for loomwork; check your library for needlepoint pattern books. You can also change the cord—maybe you want to bead a cord or use something metal. I found the leather worked well with the natural feel of these colors. This necklace has Ultrasuede as the backing; use Ultrasuede colors that complement your beads.

Looming

2 Warp your loom as described on page 20. This pattern is 15 rows of beads across, so you will need 16 warp threads. Tie 1 yd. of Nymo on the left warp thread if you're right-handed and right warp thread if you're left-handed.

Note: This piece has 51 rows of beads or weft threads. After the piece is loomed and removed from the loom, 16 of the rows will be turned to form a bail.

3 As always with loomwork, the first row is the trickiest. The beads always go under the warps with the needle passing back through the beads on top of the warps **(A)**. I find that after the second row is complete, it's easier to pull the two rows snug. Don't over tighten, but make it just snug enough that the Delicas rest peacefully next to each other. If you need to end a thread, simply tie it off on the end warp thread **(B)**, then hide the remaining thread by going through one of the rows of beads and cutting it. Add a new thread by tying onto the same warp thread and continuing; you can hide the tail by pulling it through a row of beads or tacking it along with the end warp thread.

4 After you have the loomwork done, use clear fingernail polish to coat the ends of the warp threads and the knots. This helps secure the loomwork ends once the piece is cut. With the fingernail

Materials

- 2 grams each 11º Delicas listed on pattern
- 3 grams 11º Delicas, metallic gold, for edging
- **20** 9º three-cut seed beads, brown iris, for fringe
- **12** assorted 8º seed beads
- Natural stone bead
- **2** 1-in. bone cylinder beads (Fire Mountain Gems and Beads)
- **3** ½-in. bone cylinder beads (Fire Mountain Gems and Beads)
- Bronze feather charm
- Floral charm
- Patina loop charm (etsy.com/shop/patinaworx)
- Dagger bead
- **2** bone beads for 4mm cord
- **4** metal beads for 4mm cord
- **12** 4mm assorted glass beads
- **3** 4mm pearls
- **26** 3mm copper beads
- **2** patina feathers (Fire Mountain Gems and Beads)
- **2** patina metal dangles (Fire Mountain Gems and Beads)
- **2** end caps for 4mm cord
- **2** gold split rings
- Clasp
- 16-in. 4mm leather cord
- Ultrasuede
- Tacky Glue
- Poster board

Tools

- #12 sharp beading needles for edging
- #12 long beading needles for weaving and fringe
- Nymo B
- Toothpicks
- Loom
- Masking tape
- Clear fingernail polish
- Pliers
- Scissors
- Fine-tip marker

Stitches

- Loomwork
- Simple Edging
- Fringe

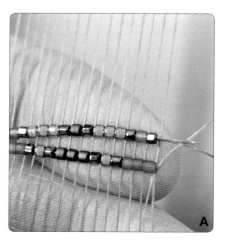

C

D

polish still a bit tacky, use masking tape to tape the ends **(C)**. Tape the warp threads so that they are in bit narrower than the loomwork so you won't see the tape once it's folded over.

5 Cut the loomwork from the warp, leaving ¾ in. of tape next to the loomwork. Cut a piece of poster board a bit narrower than the loomwork and 16 rows short of the 51 rows. Using Tacky Glue, adhere the poster board to the back of the loomwork, positioning it at the bottom of the panel. Glue the taped warp threads that are next to the poster board on top of the poster board. Also, glue the other taped warp threads onto the poster board. By gluing the tape only to the poster board and not the beads, you make a bail that the cord will fit through **(D)**. Cut a piece of Ultrasuede and glue this to the back of the piece below the bail. Leave the glued piece under a heavy flat book or cutting board for about 5 minutes so the piece dries flat.

Finishing and Fringe

6 Trim the excess Ultrasuede so it's even with the loomwork. Thread a sharp beading needle with 2 ft. of thread and knot one end. Begin Simple Edging (page 16): Sew through the inside of the Ultrasuede at the top of the loomwork where the bail starts. With the needle, sew under the side warp thread, and pull the thread tight. Pick up four metallic gold Delicas. Sew through the Ultrasuede and under the side warp thread about ⅛ in. down from where you started. Sew back up through the last bead. Pull tight, pick up three more beads, and continue Simple Edging **(E)**. When you get to the corner of the loomwork, skip one or two of the beads in a row, depending on spacing and what looks best. When edging on the ends, make sure that the needle grabs the last weaving thread in that last row and the Ultrasuede backing **(F and figure)**.

7 Edge around the pendant except the bail. End across from where you started. Tie a knot on the back of the Ultrasuede at the edge. Bring the needle through the top row of beads right before the bail. Change to a #12 beading needle, which is better for fringe.

8 Pick up a 3mm copper bead, an 8º, a 4mm bead, an 8º, a 3mm copper, four metallic gold Delicas, a patina feather, and four metallic gold Delicas. Go back through the copper and other beads already strung **(G)**. Pull snug and go through three of the loomed beads in the same row you originally came out of.

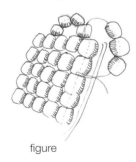

figure

E

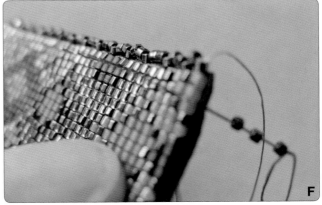

F

9 Bring the needle into the next row of loomed beads below and three rows in and come back out the side. Repeat step 7 with different beads and charms. After you have the amount of side fringe you want, knot on the back and hide the thread.

10 Using a fine-tip marker, mark dots on the back and bottom of the Ultrasuede evenly where you want the fringe. For this project I have seven fringes, so I marked both ends and the center, then two in between on each side of the center dot. This will help keep the fringe spaced evenly. Thread a new 2-ft. thread with a #12 beading needle and knot the end. Working from the back, bring the needle up through the Ultrasuede so the knot will be hidden, and exit through an end dot. Add the first row of fringe using the same technique as for the side fringe. After sewing back through the row of beads, sew through the back of the Ultrasuede, exit through the same marked dot, and pull snug. Start the next row the same way you did the first: sew through the Ultrasuede and exit through the next dot. After adding the middle fringe, sew back down through three beads and pick up three metallic gold Delicas, a patina feather, and three metallic gold Delicas. Sew back through the same three beads **(H)** and the Ultrasuede. Pull snug and start the next fringe. After the fringes are done, tie a knot on the Ultrasuede and hide the tail. Refer to the picture **(I)** to make the same fringe as I did, or change it to make it work for you. Add different charms or beads to make it your own personal peace pendant.

11 Finish the piece with a 4mm leather or metal cord. If you want to add accent beads on the cord, make sure to string the pendant and add the beads before you glue the end caps. Glue the end caps on using two-part epoxy or your glue of choice. Add the clasp using split rings. You may want to bead your own chain. It's your choice—follow your heart and make something that brings peace into your world.

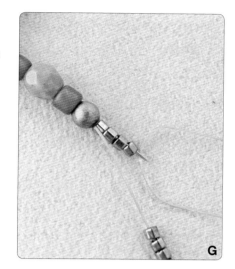
G

H

I

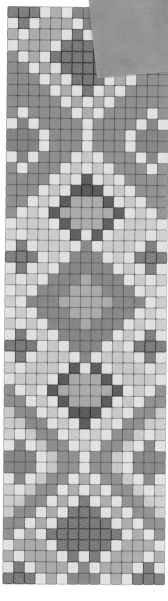

Metallic Gold DB-22 Cut

SL Teal DB-607

Matte Green DB-327

Lt. Green DB-274

SL Fuchsia DB-1340

Matte Purple DB-783

Purple Iris DB-4

Dream Box

Intuition and Dreaming

Lizard represents intuition and dream time. If you'd like to better understand your dreams, place some sea salt and a crystal in your box and keep it near your bed at night. I recycled a tiny plastic jar. I cleaned it up and made it into something worthy.

Designing

1 Choose the jar or box you wish to use. The size you find may be different than mine, so you may need to stitch your loomwork to a different length. Keep in mind that 1 in. equals 15 rows of Delicas. Remember also that beadwork placed on a curve needs to be longer than when on a flat surface, so you may need to add rows. The size of the jar will also determine the size of the beads you're using for the feet. Play with different size beads to see what looks the best and what color or material to use. I used painted wooden beads, but maybe you don't want to have feet on your box at all.

Pick an animal to rest on the top of the jar (ojime beads are great for this project). I placed the lizard on top of a rusty button. This helped elevate the lizard and gave me a smooth edge to embroider around. Look for a button that your animal can rest peacefully on. Try different animals to find the one that best fits the size of your jar or box.

The trickiest part of this project is determining the length of the loomwork. Measure the circumference of the jar lid **(A)**. Cut a piece of scrap leather equal to the circumference and height of the side of the lid. The leather stretches, so you can cut it smaller. Glue it to the side of the lid using Tacky Glue. After the glue has dried, sew the leather ends together.

The pattern is for a 1¾ in. diameter jar lid. You may need to adjust this pattern so it fits your lid and so when the loomed ends meet, the pattern matches up. If you have a piece of loomwork from another project handy, use it to help you determine the length: Place it around the leather-covered lid to see how much longer or shorter the new work needs to be.

Loomwork

2 Warp the loom as described on page 20. This pattern (page 75) is for nine beads wide, so you will need 10 warp threads. The loomwork has 89 rows. You may need to adjust this depending on the lid, as described in Designing.

3 Tie 1 yd. of thread to the edge warp thread. Follow the pattern, starting with the bottom row. Continue with the loomwork **(B)** until completed. After the loomwork is done, coat the ends of the warp threads with clear fingernail polish. While the fingernail polish is still a bit tacky, wrap the warp threads with masking tape, taping the warp threads so

Materials

- Recycled jar (1¾ in. round)
- Ojime bead animal (rings-things.com)
- 1-in. diameter (approx.) round button or platform
- 3 grams each Delica listed on pattern
- 5 grams 15° seed beads, metallic gold
- 1 gram 15° seed beads, metallic silver
- 1 gram 9° hex-cut beads, coral
- 8mm turquoise bead
- **4** 15mm wooden beads painted
- Leather scraps
- Ultrasuede
- Two-part epoxy
- Tacky Glue
- Poster board
- Fabric interfacing

Tools

- #12 sharp beading needles for edging
- #12 beading needle for weaving
- Nymo B
- Toothpicks
- Flexible measuring tape
- Loom
- Masking tape
- Clear fingernail polish
- Scissors
- Drill (optional)

Stitches

- Backstitch 4
- Backstitch 6
- Loomwork
- Tacking
- Slanted Edging

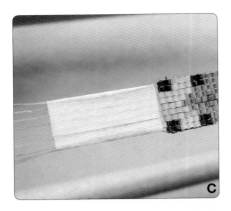

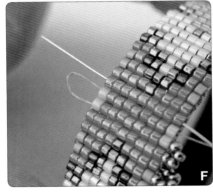

they are a bit narrower than the loomwork **(C)**. Cut the loomwork from the loom and wrap it around the lid to see if you measured correctly. If it's too long, remove the tape, take out a row, and retape. If it's too short, add a row using square stitch once it's glued to the lid.

4 To add fabric interfacing for backing, glue the taped tabs to the back of the loomwork using Tacky Glue. Cut a piece of interfacing a bit smaller than the loomwork between the tabs, and adhere with Tacky Glue. Place the work under a heavy book until the glue dries.

Attaching
5 Cut a piece of scrap leather the size of the bottom of the jar side as you did for the lid. I tacked down some 15º metallic silver beads spaced about ¼ in. apart to add texture.

6 Glue the leather to the side of the jar using Tacky Glue. After the glue has dried, stitch the leather edges together. At this stage, the top and bottom of the jar should be covered with leather and the correct length and width of loomwork

should be backed with interfacing **(D)**.

7 Glue the loomwork to the jar lid using Tacky Glue and hold it in place with masking tape until the glue dries.

8 Thread a #12 sharp with 3 ft. of thread and knot the end. Sew into the back of the leather where the loomed edges meet, sew through two beads on one end of the beadwork, and sew through two corresponding beads on the opposite side. Repeat across, weaving the two ends together **(E)**. If the loomwork is too short, add one or more rows of beadwork to one end, and then stitch the ends together.

9 After the two ends have met and are happy together, you can add some hanging edging to cover any gap between the top and bottom of the jar when closed. This edging also gives a finished look. With the needle, go through a row of beads exiting the bottom of the lid and pick up four 15º metallic gold seed beads. Now, go back up through the next row of beads heading towards the top of the box, and go back down through the next

row. Repeat all along the bottom of the lid **(F)**. Changing the number of 15º beads from four to five to six, will make the edging uneven and lacy. If you like the edging even, use the same number of beads each time.

10 Rest the bottom of the jar on a piece of Ultrasuede, trace around it using a marker, and cut out the circle. This will be the bottom of the jar; glue it in place with Tacky Glue. After the glue has set, sew the bottom Ultrasuede to the leather siding using 15º metallic gold seed beads: Thread a sharp needle with 3 ft. of thread and knot the end. Sew into the back of the leather and out the front about ⅛ in. from the edge. Pick up three 15ºs, and go through the edge of the Ultrasuede about ¼ in. away from where the needle exited the leather. Pull the thread and beads snug. Pick up three more beads and continue the Slanted Edging (page 17) all around the bottom **(G)**.

Animal Topper
11 Most Ojime beads have holes in them. If there is a hole, sew the bead to the button in addition to gluing it: Place the animal on top of the button, and, using a sharp needle, go through the hole of the animal to make a mark at the top of the button where a hole will be drilled. Drill the hole, and glue the animal to the top of the button with Epoxy. While the glue dries, place the jar lid on top of a piece of Ultrasuede and trace around it. Tie a knot at the end of 3 ft. of thread and sew up through the Ultrasuede, the button, and the animal. Pick up an 8mm turquoise bead and a seed bead, and sew back through the 8mm, animal, button, and Ultrasuede **(H)**. Retrace the thread path, and then sew up through the Ultrasuede to exit next to the button. If there is no hole in the bead, simply glue it to the button.

12 Using Backstitch 6 (page 16), work a row of 9º coral beads around the button. This is Row 1. I chose a star pattern for the top of my lid and used the same Delicas as in the loomwork. To make a star pattern, work as follows:

TOP

MIDDLE

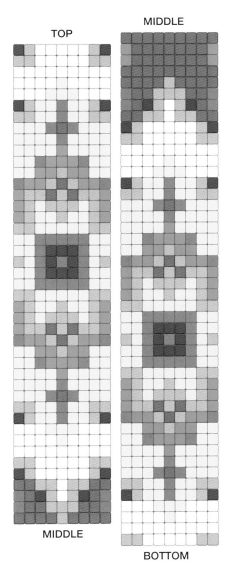

MIDDLE

BOTTOM

☐ White DB-221

▨ Metallic Gold DB-22 Cut

▨ Matte Olive DB-371

▨ Red DB-214

▨ Turquoise DB-658

▨ Dark Purple Silver Lined DB-610

☐ Light Gold DB-272

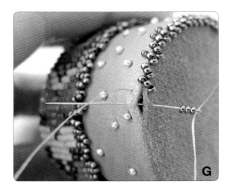
G

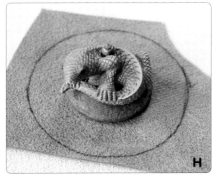
H

I

J

K

Row 2: metallic gold, two reds, two corals, two reds, and a metallic gold. Repeat for the remainder of the row.

Row 3: Bring the needle up just past a metallic gold bead, and add a metallic gold, four or five reds, a metallic gold, a matte olive green, and a metallic gold. Repeat for the rest of the row. You may need to adjust the number and color of beads so they make a star shape.

Row 4: Bring the needle up just past a metallic gold, and add a metallic gold, an olive, a turquoise, an olive, a metallic gold, and three or four reds. Repeat for the rest of the row, adjusting numbers and colors to maintain the shape.

Row 5: Exiting just past a metallic gold, add a gold, an olive, three turquoise, an olive, a gold, and two reds. Repeat for the rest of the row, adjusting numbers and colors to maintain the shape.

Row 6: Exiting just past a metallic gold, add a metallic gold, an olive, two turquoise, a white, two turquoise, an olive, a metallic gold, and a red. Repeat for the rest of the row, adding a red where the star tips come to a point and adjusting numbers and colors of beads as needed to maintain the shape.

Use Backstitch 6 for all the rows and make sure you go through the end again after you have completed it. After you have filled in the circle with your star, carefully trim **(I)**.

13 Glue the topper to the lid using Tacky Glue **(J)**. After the glue has dried, trim any excess Ultrasuede. Thread a #12 sharp beading needle with 3 ft. of thread and knot the end. Sew up through the Ultrasuede on the top of the lid. Pull the knot to hide. Pick up three 15º metallic

golds and sew under the adjacent edge warp thread on the loomwork and the Ultrasuede on the lid **(K)**. (This is the same slanted edging, but you will sew under a warp thread rather than the Ultrasuede.) Repeat along the edge of the jar lid.

Finishing

14 Now that the hard part is done, you can determine whether you want to add the wooden feet. Play with different sizes and kinds of beads. I used wooden beads painted with acrylic paint to match the Ojime. Sand the wooden beads so each has a flat surface. Glue the wooden beads to the bottom of the jar using epoxy. After the glue has dried, the box is done. Add any treasures you wish—sand is good for cleansing and dreaming.

Pawley's Peace

Honoring our Loved Ones

Honoring our family and friends who have passed not only helps us with our grief, but makes us feel as though we still have a connection with them. When Deborah Uhl approached me about making her a piece of jewelry to honor her dog, Pawley, she brought over a collection of items including Pawley's ashes, dew claws, tail tip, dog tag, and more. We combined those items plus their birthstones into a necklace that keeps the connection for Deborah. I thought it would make a perfect project to share.

Designing

1 Designing any piece starts with the components. If you're honoring a pet and you can gather some fur or the dew claws, add them to the pile. You can use a collar or tags or maybe even an old toy that you cut apart. If you're honoring a human, perhaps some hair or a piece of favorite jewelry, or maybe an old picture. Deborah also brought me Pawley's ashes and some grass where they spent their last moments together. These I incorporated in the back of the necklace behind a small piece of lizard skin, as Pawley loved to chase lizards. Use birthstones or stones that remind you of this beautiful life. Deborah choose tigereye because Pawley's eyes looked like the stone. She also picked a round picture jasper cabochon that looked like a tennis ball. Aquamarine was also incorporated in the back because it is a stone that represents water and Pawley loved the water. Deborah picked a porcelain dog face made by Laura Mears. The face was a bit different in color than Pawley's but Deborah, an artist, changed that by painting it. If you can find angelite to incorporate, I encourage it because it helps keep contact with the angelic realm.

Materials

- Laura Mears porcelain dog
- Various cabochons such as birthstones, etc.
- Brass feathers or personal charms
- Hair or fur from your loved one
- Dog or cat tag or collar
- 10 grams 15º seed beads, metallic gold
- Hank 9º three-cut seed beads, gold iris
- **2** end caps for 4mm cord
- Clasp
- 18-in. 4mm braided leather cord
- Ultrasuede for foundation and backing
- Two-part epoxy
- Tacky Glue
- Cardboard for lining

Tools

- #12 sharp beading needle
- Nymo B
- Toothpicks
- Needlenose pliers
- Scissors
- Fine-tip marker
- Ruler
- Drill (optional, if using dew claws)
- Scissors

Stitches

- Backstitch 4
- Backstitch 6
- Simple Edging

A

B

The back of the necklace contains precious elements: a pouch with ashes and grass, and angelite.

After you have gathered some components, lay them on some plain paper and move things around to see which items fit and look the best **(A)**. You may not be able to use everything you have, but you may want to incorporate some things on the back of the piece as well, such as a stone that you wish to have close to your heart.

Think about what kind of necklace you want—is it something you want to wear everyday or just for special ceremonies? Deborah wanted something she could wear almost everyday so we tried to keep it small, but still there was a lot to incorporate. The leather cord is much more comfortable for everyday use compared to a beaded collar.

Gluing and Stitching

2 After you have a general idea of where you want to place your items, cut a piece of Ultrasuede for the foundation. Always allow room for expansion of the design and cut the Ultrasuede a bit larger. Using a fine-tip marker and a ruler, draw a center line down the middle of the Ultrasuede. This will help keep the piece centered. I glued the dog tag down first using two-part epoxy and then glued the

porcelain head. I attached the head at a slight angle, giving Pawley a more real, spirited look.

3 Tie a knot at the end of 3 ft. of thread, and sew up through the Ultrasuede next to the tag. Using 15º metallic gold seed beads, work Backstitch 6 (page 16) around the main component. Next, work a row of 9º three-cut seed beads around the underside of the component **(B)**.

4 By gluing one stone, maybe two, at a time and using Backstitch 4 and 6, your piece will slowly evolve **(C)**. Keep adding your collection, fitting the puzzle together **(D)**. In my piece, the dew claws were a bit challenging. I wasn't able to get my needle through them, so I drilled a hole and that worked nicely. I used a small amount of Tacky Glue to attach the first claw **(E)**. After the glue set, I stitched the claw down through the hole I drilled and also sewed around the claw **(F)**. This was more for security reasons. I wouldn't want

to lose a claw, but I also wanted them to be removable. After the first claw was secure, I glued and stitched the second claw in place.

5 Using 9º three-cut beads, I backstitched around the claws **(G)** and filled between as needed with 9ºs and 15ºs **(H)**. This is where it really helps to have center lines marked to keep the piece straight and balanced. The piece doesn't have to be symmetrical; as in Pawley, there are different stones on each side. But, by keeping the sides lined up and even, the piece looks better. Keep filling in the piece; your heart will tell you when it's done.

Trimming and Finishing

6 Using a sharp pair of scissors, trim the excess Ultrasuede **(I)**. Don't get too close, or you may cut the threads. Leave about ⅛ in. for edging **(J)**. This is a good time to think about what kind of cord or chain you want to use. For Pawley, I used a 4mm leather cord. A beaded chain is another option.

7 The lining thickness determines how stiff the piece will be. Here, I used a cereal box. It was thick enough to hold the weight of all the components, but also easy enough to cut. Lay the finished piece on the lining, trace around it with a pencil, and then cut it ⅛ in. smaller than the

finished piece. You want it smaller so you won't have to stitch through the cardboard when you do your edging—you'll be much happier.

8 Glue the foundation to the back of the beadwork using Tacky Glue. Lay the piece flat on the table and press the beadwork onto the lining. This will help keep the beads flat and securely glued.

9 Place the beadwork on the Ultrasuede backing and trace around the beaded foundation. Cut the backing about ⅛ in. larger than the beadwork or foundation. Add ashes or other items on the back, if desired. I put Pawley's ashes and some grass into a small plastic bag. I cut a small piece of lizard skin for a pocket. I glued the edges of the lizard skin to the backing and also stitched them—nothing fancy, just a simple sewing stitch.

10 After you have attached the ashes or pouch, you can attach the cord. Mark the center of the cord with a marker to help with placement. Spread Tacky Glue onto the back of the beadwork with a toothpick, and place the cord so that the center rests in the center and top of the pendant. Put extra glue on the cord as well **(K)**, and place the backing on top. Slowly press the backing onto the lining and foundation with the cord between. Look at the front of the piece and make

sure the cord is exiting on the same side and centered where you want it. Also make sure the backing is equal and centered. After the glue has dried, trim any excess backing so it's the same size as the foundation.

11 After the piece is trimmed, stitch Simple Edging (page 16) all around the piece **(L)**. Edge around the cord, and tack it to the backing where possible. You don't need to stitch through the cord **(M)**. Trim the cord to the desired length, glue on the end caps, and add the clasp.

Fringe

12 Plan your fringe below the finished pendant **(N)** first. This way you can move things around and see what looks and

J

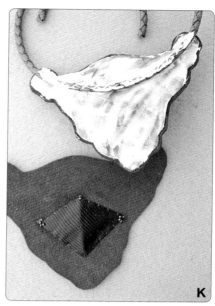

K

L

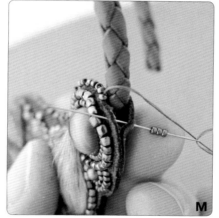

M

N

feels the best. Deborah wanted to have some of Pawley's tail fur and her own hair together. I tied the fur and hair together using beading thread and a few knots (**O**). I then found an old leather piece and glued the bundle together. A bicone, large-hole bead, or end cap would serve the same purpose.

13 To attach the fringe, tie a knot at the end of 2 ft. of thread and attach a #12 beading needle. Bring the needle up between the foundation and backing and through the back, a bead-length away from the middle. Pick up four 9ºs, the center dangle, and four 9ºs. Sew through the front of the foundation and out through the back right next to the first row on the other side of the middle. Now pick up four more 9ºs and go through the

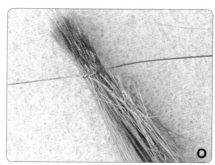

O

dangle again. Pick up four 9ºs and sew through the foundation front, exiting the backing. Pull the dangle snug and repeat the fringe on either side (**P**). Work one more fringe on this side.

14 Repeat the last two fringes on the other side of the center dangle.

P

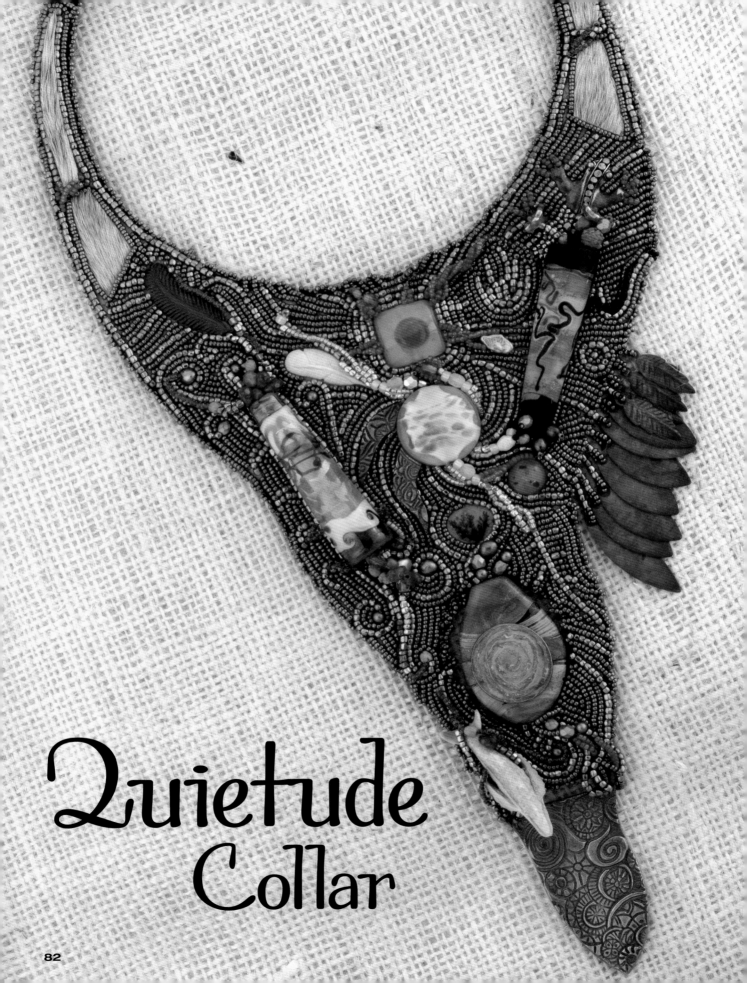

Quietude
Collar

Grounding, Energy, Cleansing, Space, and Your Life's Journey

There are many ways to bring the four elements into your beadwork: Use natural stones, reference animals and colors associated with the element you honor, and reflect its gifts, thus bringing forth its energy and sharing it with the world. This piece was a collaboration with Louise Little and her beautiful glass beads, and was inspired by a juried show with a Four Elements theme.

Designing

1 Gather your materials. Pick something to represent each element and a main central bead which reflects the spiral of life, your personal journey (or not). Also pick smaller stones and animals that represent each element. (To find out more about representations of the elements, see pages 24–45.)

2 Using a plain piece of paper and a compass, draw a 5½-in. diameter circle. Mark a center line from the top of the circle to the bottom of the paper. You may need to adjust the size of the circle depending on the size collar you wish to make.

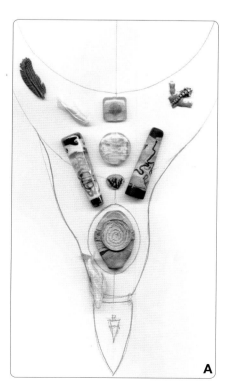

A

3 Now you have your "canvas" on which to lay out your stones and glass beads. Play with arrangements to see where items fit the best. I placed the main spiral bead in the center. This central bead was so beautiful I decided to make it visible from both sides. After everything is in place, draw the lines of the outside of the collar. Be creative with the shape—it doesn't have to be perfectly symmetrical **(A)**. I added metal drops on one side to help balance the design. You may want to add fringe to the collar; I made a medallion from silver precious metal clay, but you may find something else that works just as well.

4 After you have a pattern drawn and an idea of where things will be placed, take a photo or sketch around the pieces so you will remember your plan. After you start beading, things may change—which is fine! This is a work in progress. Cut out the pattern and see how it fits around your neck. Now is the time to make any adjustments. Keep in mind the clasp will require several inches at the back. Trace around the pattern onto a piece of Lacy's Stiff Stuff or Ultrasuede using a marker. Make sure to transfer the center line, too, as this will be a helpful reference.

Gluing and Stitching

5 It helps to glue the first stone or bead in the center and work your way out rather than starting on one side of the collar. Using the center line for guidance, glue the first bead with epoxy. I started with the sun bead. If you are using beads rather than stones for your elements, stitch them down to the foundation for added security.

Materials

- **4** beads to represent the four elements (desertbloomdesigns.com)
- Bead representing the spiral of your life's journey
- Various stones, animals, and beads representing the four elements
- Various larger and colorful complementary beads
- Fur or leather if available
- Metal medallion
- **12** brass patina drops (item #D40-3419FX firemountaingems.com)
- Hank 9º three cut seed beads, gold iris
- 25 grams 15º seed beads, metallic gold
- **2** clasp hooks
- **2** figure-8 connectors
- Lacy's Stiff Stuff
- Ultrasuede
- Thin cardboard for lining
- Two-part epoxy glue
- Tacky Glue

Tools

- #12 sharp beading needles
- Nymo B
- Toothpicks
- Marker
- Ruler
- Compass
- Scissors

Stitches

- Backstitch 4
- Backstitch 6
- Simple Edging
- Fringe
- Twisting
- Tacking

6 Two sizes of seed beads and two shades of gold complements the stones and creates wonderful patterns in the embroidery. Work in Backstitch 6 (page 16) to begin framing your elements. I embroidered a star shape around my sun bead. I began with 9º three-cuts for the first row. The second row is a repeating pattern of three 9ºs, and a 15º. In each subsequent row, I picked up more 15ºs and omitted 9ºs to create the star.

Use a marker to draw lines that your embroidery will follow. For the air bead, I wanted swirling lines **(B)**.

7 If you want the spiral bead to rotate freely within the beadwork, cut that area out of the foundation now **(C)**. Hold the bead in the center to make sure it has enough clearance to move freely.

8 Continue adding to the collar using Backstitch 6 and switching to Backstitch 4 for tight turns **(D)**.

9 As the piece evolves, you may want to mark some lines to help with placement of stones or other items **(E)**. This is also a good time to figure out the clasp. Use a clasp that's already made, or make your own. I made my own using a clay bear cabochon I had along with some azurite stones on either side. The clasp is a mini version of the whole collar and should be just as special **(F)**. Lay the clasp where it will go **(G)** and adjust the length of the collar where needed.

10 If you're incorporating fur, cut it into the desired shape and glue it down with Tacky Glue **(H)**. After the glue has dried, stitch the fur along the edges. Backstitch a row of beads along the fur and treat it just as you would a cabochon.

11 With only gold beads in the background, colors added on top will really pop. For example, use some twisted red for the fire elements or black to tie in the earth bead **(I)**. Create a three-

dimensional feel by adding different sized beads exiting from the larger element beads **(J)**. By adding the colored and larger beads, your piece comes alive and complements the patterns. Use tacking and twisting stitches (p. 18).

Trimming and Finishing

12 Trim the piece, being careful not to cut any threads. After trimming, you'll have an idea of what the collar will look like. This is a good time to see where you may need to add more color or depth **(K)**.

Find a piece of cardboard for the lining. You don't want it to be too thick or you will have a stiff collar; cereal boxes or poster board work well. Cut the lining ⅛ in. smaller than the collar and clasp. Lay it on the back of the collar to check that the lining is cut properly. If not, once the piece is glued together it will be hard to edge if you have to stitch through cardboard. Before gluing the lining to the back of the clasp, sew a figure-8

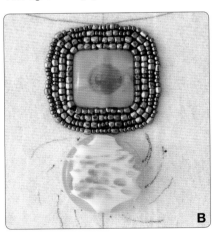

B

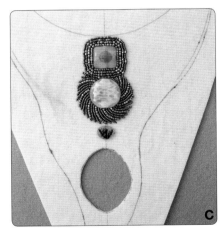

C

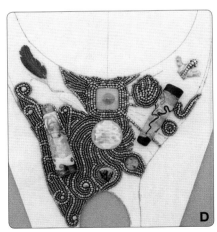

D

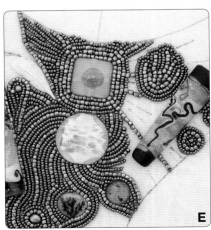

E

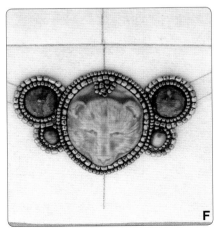

F

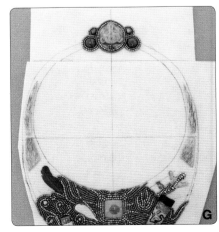

G

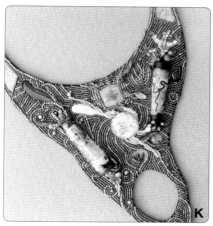

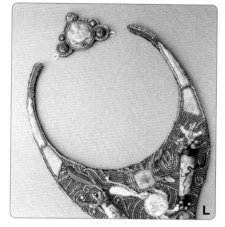

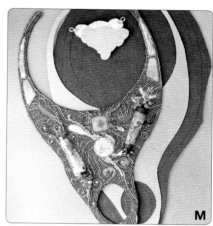

connector on either side of the clasp. The hooks from the collar will hook onto these, making a clasp **(L)**.

13 Spread Tacky Glue on the cardboard lining. Place the lining on a flat tabletop, and carefully press the beadwork onto the lining, making it flat and happy. Use Ultrasuede for backing the collar and the clasp **(M)**. Spread Tacky Glue on the back of the collar lining (already glued in place). Glue the collar to the back of the Ultra-suede, pressing the beads down on a flat surface. After the glue has set, trim any excess Ultrasuede. Using a marker the same color as the Ultrasuede, mark the foundation so the white is not so visible. Repeat with the clasp portion.

14 Using 15º metallic gold seed beads, edge the clasp with Simple Edging (page 16).

15 Sew two hooks to each end of the collar **(N)**. These will hook onto the clasp.

Edge with Simple Edging and 15º metallic gold seed beads. If you have a hole in the middle for the floating bead, make sure to edge around that as well.

16 To attach the floating spiral bead, exit the beadwork at the bottom of the hole and pick up the spiral bead. Add some accent beads, if needed, to center the bead in the space and sew the beadwork at the top of the hole. Retrace the thread path several times for security.

17 If you're using a medallion, sew it to the bottom of the collar. Go through one or two of the rows of beads embroidered on the collar and continue the row onto the medallion. I added a bone whale to the bottom of my collar to look like it was floating down onto the medallion. I drilled holes in the whale and stitched it down and around its fins to keep it in place.

18 Add some fringe if you like. The collar I made was not symmetrical, so by adding

some metal drops to one side, the piece became more balanced.

This is your collar and your journey. It should be as individual as you are. By making this special piece, you are honoring the four elements and raising the consciousness of the universe. Wear it with pride and confidence.

Grace's Angel Collar

"Believing people can soar beyond ordinary life."

— Fools Crow—Lakota

Materials
- Cabochons you wish to use
- Strand 9º three-cut seed beads, gold iris
- 5 grams 15º seed beads, metallic gold
- 5 grams 15º seed beads, metallic silver
- 20 grams 15º seed beads, background color
- **4–5** shades 15º seed beads for feathers
- 5 grams 15º or smallerseed beads, black
- **2** 2mm onyx beads or cabochons for eyes
- **2** vintage buttons
- Various beads for fringe bottoms
- 4mm Czech fire-polished beads for loops
- Feather dangle (Fire Mountain Gems and Beads)
- Clasp
- Ultrasuede for backing and foundation
- Poster board for lining and graph
- Two-part epoxy
- Tacky Glue
- Tracing paper

Tools
- #12 sharp beading needle
- #15 beading needle
- #12 beading needle
- Nymo B
- Toothpick
- Scissors
- Ruler
- Printer
- Fine-tip marker

Stitches
- Backstitch 4 and 6
- Simple Edging
- Twisted Fringe

Miracles Do Happen

I wanted to make a collar with hummingbirds but was unsure of what color to make them. I have always thought white hummingbirds would be beautiful, but I didn't think they even existed. A week before I was to start this project, I was having lunch on the deck when a flash of white shot out of the trees and landed on my feeder. A white hummingbird! We had to euthanize our sweet dog Grace a week before, and I believe she sent this angel to let us know she made it to doggie heaven. This collar might take you awhile, but let the magic and miracles of your life guide you as you work. You can embroider any animal you wish. Simply find a good picture and either trace or copy it to tracing paper which will be glued to your suede as a pattern.

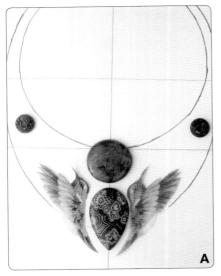

A

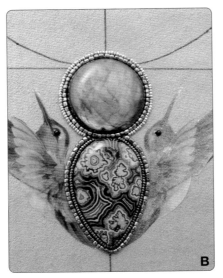

B

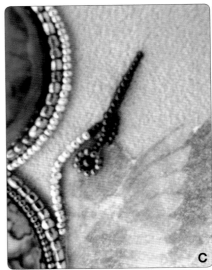

C

D

E

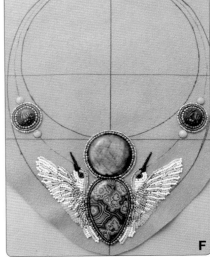

F

Designing

1 Use the collar template (page 91) to get started. Enlarge it to 183%, cut it out, and try it on. The inside dimension is 5¼ in. If the opening needs to be larger, use a compass to get the perfect curve. This pattern is a simple one that can be changed as needed. After you have a pattern that works, trace around it on a piece of poster board. Make sure to mark the center lines, as they will help guide you throughout the project.

2 Copy a hummingbird pattern onto tracing paper with a copier or by hand. Greeting cards and calendars are a great place to look for animals and birds you may want to use. Use a copier to size

them as needed. It works best to tape a piece of tracing paper to an 8½x11-in. sheet of paper, make the copy, and then remove the tracing paper.

3 Gather the cabochons you want to use and start placing them onto the poster board pattern. Cut out the hummingbirds and place them on either side of the stones **(A)**. Tracing paper is transparent, so you can use the same pattern and have a left and right hummingbird. Also, it's thin enough that you can stitch right through it. Play around with the placement until you have a design that works for you. The collar pattern is just a guide. Your cabochons and hummingbirds will most likely extend below the bottom line.

4 Your hummingbirds don't have to be white—they can be any color you wish. Pick complementary stones and beads. My background color changed completely from what I had originally envisioned. Choose an Ultrasuede foundation and

backing that will also complement the stones and beads. I find that tan and beige foundations work well with most beads, but the darker the Ultrasuede, the harder it is to use guidelines. Cut the poster board pattern and transfer it onto the Ultrasuede foundation. Make sure to transfer the center guidelines as well.

Gluing and Stitching

5 Using the center lines as guides, glue the center or largest cabochon first using two-part epoxy. After the glue has set, stitch one row of 9º three-cut gold iris beads around the cabochon using Backstitch 6 (page 16).

6 With epoxy, adhere the next stone above or below the first stone and next to the row of beads. You don't need to knot the thread every time you glue a cabochon as long as the thread is close to your work. Stitch a row of 15º metallic golds (or your choice of beads) around the second cabochon. Add as many rows as you wish. I added just two to keep the hummingbirds close to the center.

7 Using rubber cement, glue the two tracing paper hummingbirds next to the last row of beads where you want them to rest. I find rubber cement works best for this, as it doesn't curl the paper **(B)**.

8 If you are using a 2mm cabochon for the eye, cut and remove the tracing paper where the eye will be. It's better to glue the cabochon directly to the foundation. (If you don't have a cabochon and are using a bead, just stitch it directly through the paper.) Attach the cabochon eye with epoxy. After the glue dries, stitch a row of 15º or smaller metallic gold beads with Backstitch 4 around the eye. Use the 15º or smaller black beads for the beak **(C)**. Stitch right on top of the tracing paper; you will never see it once it's beaded.

9 Use the lines and colors of the copied pattern to help you with the placement of the beads. By using different shades of white and following the lines, you will create feathers **(D)**. If you are making a green hummingbird, use shades of green rather than white. If you want the colored throat of most hummingbirds, add it below the eye.

10 Take your time. Play that book on CD. Your second hummingbird will be easier than the first but I bet you won't want to redo the first one. Make the backs of the hummingbirds snug next to the rows of beads around your cabochon so they are one with each other **(E)**.

11 Using epoxy and following the guidelines, glue on the two buttons or stones you have picked out that will rest on each side of the collar. I also added a guideline marking the center of the sides all the way to the front. This will help not only with gluing buttons but also with the background stitching.

12 After the epoxy has set, add three rows of beads around the glued buttons and then glue two smaller cabochons next to the third row of beads on either side, using the guidelines for placement **(F, G)**.

13 Use Backstitch 4 and Backstitch 6 to add beads of your choice and rows of beads around the smaller stones. The guidelines will help with placement. Use bead colors that complement the hummingbirds **(H)**.

14 With all the stones and hummingbirds in place and beaded, move on to the background. Pick a bead color that will make the hummingbirds pop but also complement the stone colors and beads. I placed different bead colors in the background to see what they would look like **(I)**. Its easier to lay the beads down first than to stitch them and realize they aren't working. After placing a dark color and a gray iridescent color, I decided to go with something completely different—matte gold—a much better choice.

15 Stitching the background is another long process, so take a breath and start the next chapter of your book on CD. Use the center line as a guide. Start the first row of beads next to the last row by the main cabochon—this will give a slight curve. Stitch a row from the center line to the edge (if the hummingbird's head is where the guideline is, just imagine the line exists behind it but don't stitch). Stitch rows from each side to the middle, alternating as you go **(J and figure 1)**. Use Backstitch 6 and always go back through the rows. I know, I know. It's a hassle. The rows will be much stronger and smoother for the extra time spent.

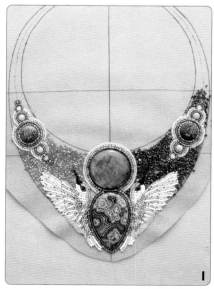

16 Work to the end alternating from one side to the next as you go. The rows will get smaller as you approach the end. I placed a small copper bead with a row of 15º metallic gold seed beads around it at the end to help keep the design of the piece whole and tie it together **(K)**. Repeat to fill in the background on the other side.

Trimming and Finishing

17 When the background is finished **(L)** carefully trim the piece, leaving approximately ¹⁄₁₆ in. of foundation. If the foundation and the marked line are visible, no worries—we'll cover it up in a future step. If it really bothers you, wash it away with a wet cotton swab.

18 Trim the poster board pattern you made earlier by ⅛ in. and use it for the lining. Adhere the lining to the back of the beadwork with Tacky Glue. Spread the glue with a toothpick on the lining rather than to the back of the beadwork. After gluing, lay the lining on a flat surface and press the beadwork to the lining so the back of the beadwork lies flat and happy.

19 Lay the work on top of the Ultrasuede for the backing and trim a piece approximately 1 in. larger than needed. Use Tacky Glue to adhere the work to the Ultrasuede. Spread the glue to the back of the beadwork and lining and position it on top of the backing. On a flat surface, press the beadwork so it lies flat.

20 When the Tacky Glue has set, trim the excess Ultrasuede. Using 15º metallic gold seed beads, work Simple Edging (page 16) to edge the piece. Start at the clasp end. To end and add thread as you go, tie knots on the back near the edge. When adding thread, hide the knot between the backing and the foundation.

21 Stitch on the clasp. With the needle exiting the back on one end, pick up four 15º metallic golds, half of the clasp, and four 15ºs. Sew into the front of the bead-work opposite the starting point. This time, bring the needle out the back and next to the first row. Repeat 3–4 times. Go through the rows a few times for extra strength **(M)**. Repeat on the other end.

22 To hide the Ultrasuede and any guideline markings remaining along the edge, weave in and out of the back-ground beads along the edge, to give the background a feathered look: At the clasp end, sew into the middle of the beaded background and exit the last row of background beads. Pick up three

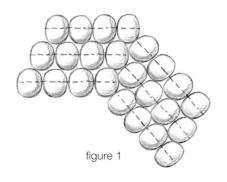

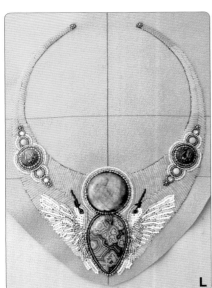

figure 1

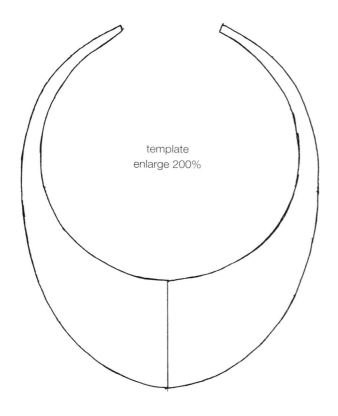

template
enlarge 200%

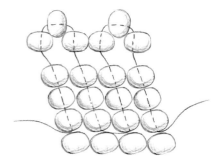

figure 2

background-color beads and sew into the end of the three background beads in the next row. Turn and sew through the end three beads in the next row. Pick up three beads and repeat along the edging **(N and figure 2)**. Not only does this cover the foundation Ultrasuede, but it also gives the piece a beautiful feathered edge.

23 Now it's time for fringe. I added nine strands of twisted fringe (page 22). Add any kind of fringe you want or none at all.

24 Let's add some loops in the front to extend the hummingbirds' tails and give some added depth. Use beads the same color as the tail. Sew through the beadwork to exit a top row of tail-feather beads. Pick up approximately 16 15ºs, a 3mm fire-polished bead, and 16 15ºs. Go into the tail-feather bead on the opposite side. You may need to add or omit 15ºs so the loop is even on each side. Repeat with the next row of tail feathers, and add a few more 15ºs and fire-polished beads so the loop is longer. Repeat until you

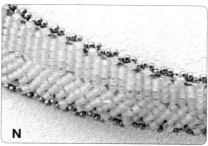

have the desired amount of loops. Add a feather charm on the bottom loop—it's your special piece so make it your own **(O)**.

25 To finish my piece, I added an angelite bead on the back with two rows of beading around it. I glued it on a separate piece of Ultrasuede and beaded around it. Then, I glued it to the back of my piece with Tacky Glue **(P)**. Angelite is the stone that helps us be conscious and have contact with the angelic realm. In this I feel I have a connection with Grace, my sweet dog and companion for nine years. I hope you too can make a special hummingbird piece that brings you years of miracles.

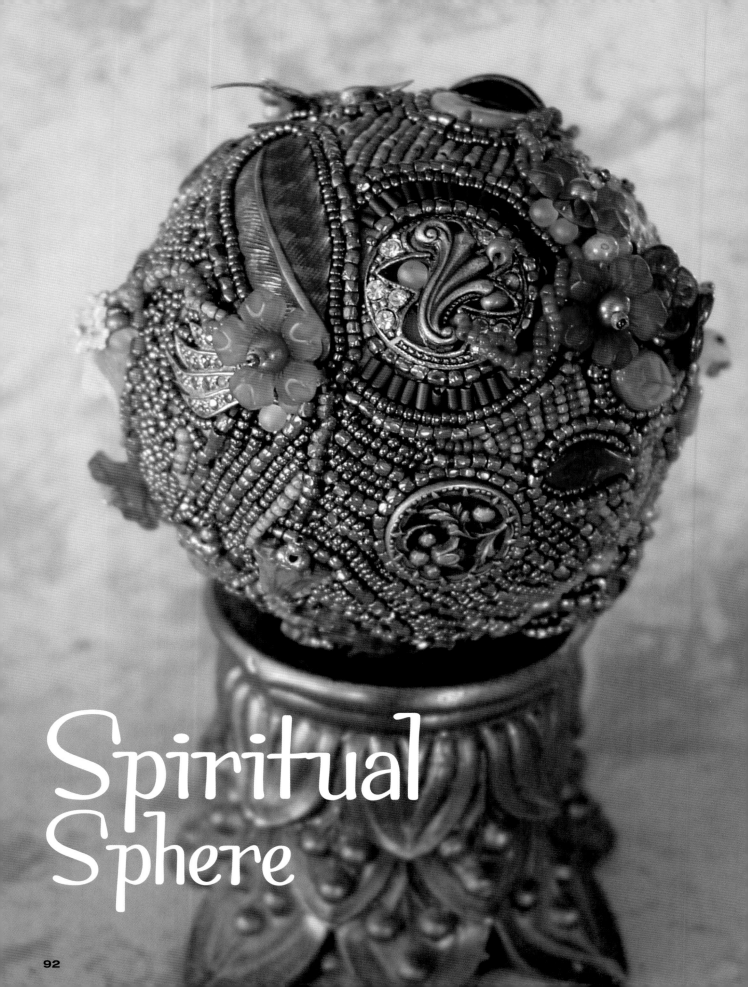

Spiritual
Sphere

Personal Growth and Balance

Don't be intimidated by this project or expect to finish it in a weekend. Rather, embrace the challenge and take time to grow with it. Take a season or even a year to reflect and gather. A theme, such as a family tree, grandmother's buttons, or your animal totems and stones, helps the planning. Balance your treasures so the sphere can rest on any side. Most of all, enjoy the time beading and growing with the piece—a time to perhaps reflect upon your life and your loved ones. The older we get, the more wisdom we have. Life seems to be more balanced somehow. Our spiritual path grows as do our children.

Materials

- Various cabochons, buttons, animals, old jewelry, pictures, miniatures, metal components, etc.
- Various beads of all sizes, shapes, and colors including pearls, leaves, flowers, daggers, etc.
- Hank 9º three-cut seed beads, gold iris
- 20 grams 15º seed beads, metallic gold
- 3-in. foam ball
- Ultrasuede
- Masking tape
- Two-part epoxy glue
- Tacky Glue

Tools

- #12 sharp beading needles
- #12 beading needles
- Nymo B
- Toothpicks
- Cotton swabs
- Marker
- String
- Scissors
- Needlenose pliers
- Masking tape
- Utility knife

Stitches

- Backstitch 4
- Backstitch 6
- Twisting
- Tacking

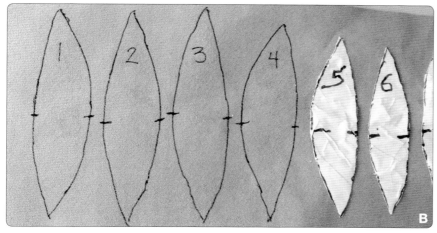

Designing

1 Gather everything that you may want to use. It's better to have too much than too little (I'm sure that won't be a problem). Because you'll be gluing items to a curved sphere, you may need to bend them or use items with a natural curve.

Prepare the Sphere for Beading

2 I've used a 3-in. foam ball but you can use a 6-in. or larger ball. Cover the ball with a few layers of masking tape, keeping it as smooth and wrinkle-free as possible.

3 Pin the center of a 12-in. piece of string to the ball. Wrap it around, keeping it centered. Wrap each end around the ball twice to create eight sections (like a basketball). Use a marker to trace along the string. Number each section on the top **(A)**. Mark horizontal lines to help with placement later when you sew them together. Remove the string.

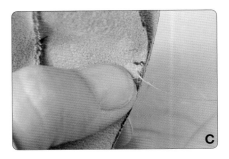

Fortune Teller
**A 6 in. sphere made in 2009
by Heidi Kummli**

4 Use a utility knife to cut the tape sections along the vertical lines and peel them off. Re-tape the ball to help keep little flakes of foam from getting on the piece and the work space.

5 Tape the cut sections onto a piece of Ultrasuede and trace around them. Number the tops and mark the centers **(B)**.

6 Cut out the marked sections, and sew them together. Using the center lines, start in the middle and work your way out to either end **(C)**. Keep the numbers in order and on top. Sew 1–4 and 5–8 to create two halves. Try them on the ball **(D)** and see how they fit; you want them snug. They may not touch completely— this is OK; they won't be perfect. I work on one side of the ball at a time, but you may want to work on both sides.

Gluing and Stitching
7 Glue the first item in place using epoxy. Choose a heavier piece. Glue it in the middle of one of the halves so you can work towards the edges.

8 Stitch around the piece with Backstitch 4 or 6 (page 16). Glue on another piece and start growing your beaded path **(E)**. Glue some of your objects over the edge to help make it hard to find the seam later on and to help space the pieces evenly **(F)**.

9 Keep going. Take your time and slowly add more items and fill in between them. Use the different backgrounds described on page 19 to help fill in.

10 Use clothespins or the masking tape roll to help hold the ball steady when gluing items **(G)** and to hold them in place until the glue dries. Your items are being glued to a curve, so if you are using something metal, you may need to bend it.

11 Mark and add lines where an item might cross the edge **(H)**. Having pieces cross over will help tie the two sides together.

12 Work the beads as closely to the edge as you can to have less to compensate for later **(I)**. When you start working on the opposite side where an element is crossing, follow the lines you drew and stitch a row of beads as though the piece was glued there. When you glue the two halves together, if all was planned well, they should meet up.

13 After the two sides are complete, put them on the ball and see how things fit. You may need to add a row or remove one. If all looks good, now is a great time to add some twisted rows or tack some beads where you may need more. I added some twisted rows of red beads to pull the piece together. I wanted the red to flow throughout the piece, making it look planned even though it wasn't **(J)**.

Finishing
14 After the two sides are done, it's time to glue. It's best to have the time to sew the sides together while the glue is still

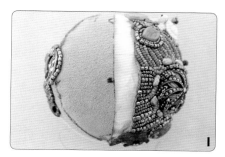
I

tacky so it can help hold the sides, rather than glue and then wait a week to finish.

15 Spread Tacky Glue with a cotton swab on the inside of one of the halves, working the glue all the way to the edge. For overhanging pieces such as the bear, glue that half on last to keep it on top **(K)**.

16 Thread a #12 beading needle with 2 ft. of beading thread and knot the end. Sew up through the backing along one edge, exiting one of the rows with the needle pointed toward the edge. Pick up the number of beads needed to reach the opposite side—preferably the same beads so they match. You're filling in between the rows and before you know it, you won't be able to find the seam **(L)**.

17 When you get to the other side, sew in to a few beads on the opposite side and then sew into the row next to it. Follow that row of beads to the edge. Repeat all along the edges to bring them together.

18 There may be spots where the beads don't match up. That's OK. Just go with the flow and put a row on top if needed— no one will be able to tell. You may also come across rows that meet perfectly and don't need any added beads. Go through the rows anyway to help them flow together. You may find it challenging to keep your grip on the needle. This is where patience and needlenose pliers come in handy.

19 You may stitch all around the seam and find you have a few spots that aren't perfect, or maybe you just want to add something else. This is where a simple pin comes in handy: Add a flower bead, pearl, or sequin. Add a drop of glue to the end of the pin and stick it into the sphere **(M)**. Problem solved.

J

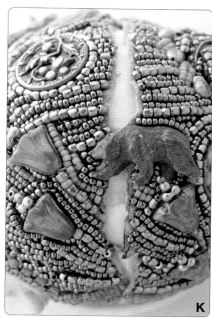
K

L

M

20 As with any large piece you make, it seems to get more difficult as you get to the end because the piece gets heavier and tricker to hold. Be patient, take breaks, and don't forget to breathe. You will make it to the end. It's fun to look for different things that will hold the sphere— candle holders work well, as do napkin rings. You can also make a beaded chain and hang your sphere at the window. The whole time I worked on this project, I made sure it was up high so my new puppy wouldn't think it was a toy ball. I made it to the end and you will too. I hope the journey was fun and you discovered things about yourself you didn't even know. I am sure you are more patient then when you started.

Althea
Earrings
by Sherry Serafini

Solace and Peace

Althea is a Greek word for healing. For me, beading is a healing, meditative process. All the cares of the world are thrown aside when I create, so it felt right to name my project for Heidi's book something related to healing. Choose stones you are drawn to and get carried away in your creative self.

Materials

- **2** 28x10mm oval stones, palmwood
- **2** 20x20mm triangle-shaped river jasper
- 2 grams 15º seed beads, 14K gold (A)
- 3 grams 15º seed beads, matte black (B)
- 1 gram 15º seed beads, bronze (C)
- **2** 2x3 in. pieces Ultrasuede
- **2** 5mm sequins, crystal AB
- **4** 3mm copper pearls
- **2** 7-in. pieces of chain
- **2** 5-in. pieces of chain
- **2** 3½ in. pieces of chain
- Pair of lever back earrings
- **2** pieces 2x3 in. beading foundation (Lacys Stiff Stuff)
- Adhesive

Tools
- Nymo B
- #13 beading needle
- Scissors

Stitches
- Backstitch

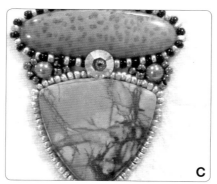

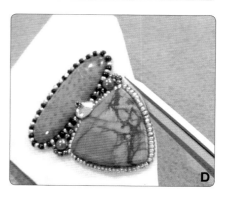

1 Glue the stones to the beading foundation. Leave space (two seed beads wide) between the stones **(A)**. Dry.

2 Thread a needle with 2 yds. of beading thread and knot the end. Backstitch a row of A beads around the triangular stone.

3 Backstitch a row of alternating A and B beads around the oval stone. Backstitch a 3mm pearl between the two stones above each triangle stone corner **(B)**.

4 Fill in the white area with C beads. You may have to stitch some of the beads sideways to fit them in. Backstitch a row of C beads around the pearls.

5 Sew up through the center space between the two stones and pick up a sequin and a C bead.

6 Skip the 15º, and sew back through the sequin. Retrace the thread path for strength **(C)**.

7 Exit the back, tie a knot, and trim the thread.

8 Carefully cut the excess beading foundation away from the beadwork **(D)**.

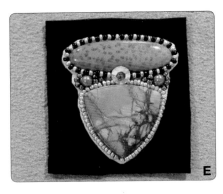

E

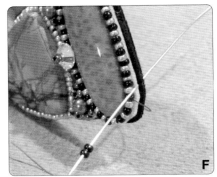

F

G

H

19 Find the edge bead on this side of the oval stone that corresponds with the one that is attached to the 3-in. chain on the first side, and sew out through that bead. Pick up the remaining end of the 3-in. chain and sew back down through the edge bead. Work as in step 16 to attach the remaining end link of the 5-in. and the 7-in. chains. They now hang as fringe.

20 Here comes the fun part. Flip the piece over so the oval is at the top. The chains that looked lovely hanging as fringe now look more interesting cascading over the tops of the cabochons.

21 Sew through the beading foundation to find your way to the top center three edge beads. Pick up three Bs, a C, the loop of the earring finding, a C, and three Bs. Skip over the center bead and exit the third bead over.

22 Sew up through the edge bead directly beside the one you just came through.

23 Pick up four Bs. Pass through the C, the loop of the earring finding, and the next C. Pick up four Bs, and sew through the edge bead on the opposite side.

24 Sew through all the Bs supporting the earring again for strength.

25 Make a second earring.

9 Glue the beadwork to the Ultrasuede backing. Keep the adhesive about ⅛ in. from the edge **(E)**.

10 Flip the piece so the oval cabochon is at the bottom. Thread a needle on 1 yd. of thread and knot the end. Sew between the layers of the beading foundation and the backing at the bottom left or right of the piece (near the oval cabochon) and pull, hiding the knot.

11 Sew through the edge of the bead-work to anchor the thread. With the needle exiting the edge, pick up two Bs and sew down through the beading foundation and the Ultrasuede **(F)**.

12 Before tightening the stitch, sew up through the second 15° strung. The first stitch is the only time you pick up two beads.

13 Pick up one B, sew down through the beading foundation and the Ultrasuede, and sew back up through the bead just added. Continue around the entire piece until you meet the first bead you

anchored. Sew through the first bead, connecting the last to the first.

14 Sew out through the edge bead you started with. Pick up the end link of a 7-in. chain, and sew back down through the same edge bead you exited **(G)**.

15 Sew out through the edge bead directly beside it, working inward toward the center of the oval stone.

16 Pick up a 5-in. chain and sew back through the same edge bead you just exited, and sew out through the next edge bead.

17 Work as in step 16, picking up a 3-in. chain.

18 Sew through the beading foundation to get to the other side of the oval stone **(H)**.

Gallery

We create beautiful things because
beauty is what we see.
We use our hands that are guided by
good thoughts.
What we make holds our feelings.
The creator has given us special gifts,
we share them with you.
— Howard Rainer

↑ SHERRY SERAFINI
Soul of a Gypsy 2011
Bead embroidery using seed beads, cabochons,
Ultrasuede.
(Photo by the artist)

← JANIS HOLLER
Portal 2010
Polymer clay.
(Photo by Heidi Kummli)

Gallery

← HEIDI KUMMLI
Shapeshifter 2010
Bead embroidery and braiding using seed beads, bone clone owl skull, and glass eye.
(Photo by the artist)

↓ HEIDI KUMMLI
Rusty Wolf 2010
Bead embroidery using seed beads, rusty washer, bone wolf, and turquoise cabochons.
(Photo by the artist)

← LAURA HUMENIK
Mario 2011
Bead embroidery using glass clay, moukite and wood beads.
(Photo by Sarajane Helm)

→ **LAURA HUMENIK**
Jewel 2011
Bead embroidery using bone face and glass beads.
(Photo by Sarajane Helm)

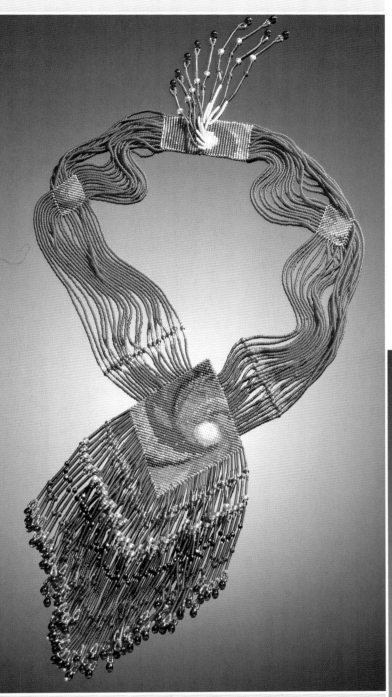

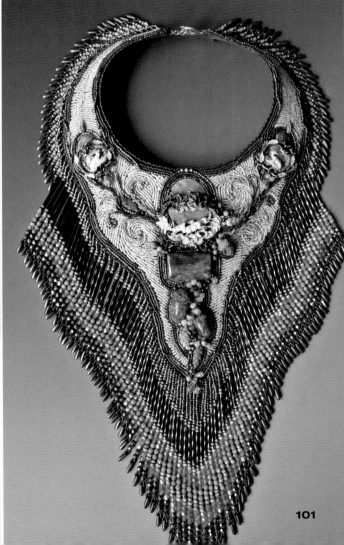

↑ **MARGIE DEEB**
Into the Vortex 1999
Split weave loom woven.
(Photo by Neil Moore)

→ **HEIDI KUMMLI**
Black Forest 2010
Bead embroidery using Black Forest bone carving.
(Photo by the artist)

Gallery

↓ FARESS CROMBE

Travel Through the Looking Glass 2011

Bead embroidery using seed beads and various goodies.

(Photo by Laura Crombe)

↑ MARGIE DEEB

The Light of Hope 2011

Bead embroidery.

(Photo by the artist)

↓ FRIEDA BATES

Patience 1999

Loomwork using 15º seed beads, 14mm rondelles, 4mm smooth rounds, 4mm crystals, 3mm faceted rounds.

(Photo by Margie Deeb)

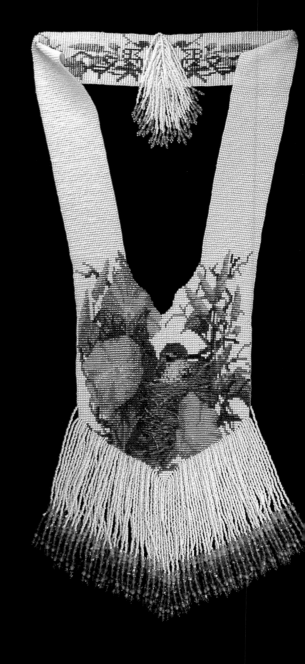

← **DIANE HYDE**
Frog in the Moment 2011
Bead embroidery, fringing using seed beads, brass vintage components.
(Photo by the artist)

↓ **HEIDI KUMMLI**
Earth Spirit 2011
Bead embroidery, webbing, twisted fringe using seed beads, leather, ermine tails, and mesh from an old purse.
(Photo by the artist)

← **HEIDI KUMMLI**
Bite Me 2011
Bead embroidery using turquoise, jasper, fur, bone bear.
(Photo by the artist)

Gallery

↓ EDDA BLUME
Zaltana 2005
Bead embroidery using jasper, ojime horses, seed and Czech beads, felt, and leather backing.

(Photo by the artist)

↓ HEIDI KUMMLI
Vintage Button with Bone Face 2010
Bead embroidery, vintage buttons, bone face, seed beads, and 4mm beads.

(Photo by the artist)

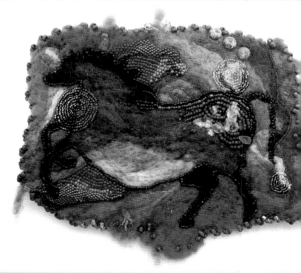

↑ ALISON DEARBORN
Abundance 2011
Hand needle felting with bead embroidery using wool roving, seed beads, and accent beads.

(Photo by Heidi Kummli)

↓ JANET KAY SKEEN
Cora's Flower Garden 2011
Bead embroidery using various glass seed beads, vintage and new ribbons, and lampworked beads by Kim Fields on suede and fabric.
(Photo by Heidi Kummli)

↓ SHERRY SERAFINI
Solitude 2011
Bead embroidery using seed beads, cabochons, Ultrasuede.
(Photo by the artist)

← JOANN PATTERSON-LAVELY
Spirit of the Sea 2011
Improvisational bead embroidery using assorted beads on fabric.
(Photo by Ken Sanville)

Gallery

↓ VICTORIA PEARMAN

Beech ligaii ma-e Navajo a Wise and Noble Messenger 2009

Bead embroidery with brick stitch and fringe, 11º and 15º seed beads, turquoise, coral, metal fox head.

(Photo by Heidi Kummli)

↓ MICHELINE BRIERRE

Sea and Sky Totem 2011

Beading on fiber using beads, gemstones, and bone.

(Photo by Barry D. Kaplan)

↓ HEIDI KUMMLI AND SHERRY SERAFINI
Migration 2010
Bead embroidery and peyote stitch using various cabochons, metal, clay, and beads.
(Photo by Larry Sanders)

↓ MICHELINE BRIERRE
In the Dream Time 2011
Beading on fiber with beads, gemstones, bone.
(Photo by Barry D. Kaplan)

← FARRESS CROMBE
I'm Nuts-oh Crazy About You 2011
Bead embroidery using family photo, agate, seed beads, and real acorns.
(Photo by Laura Crombe)

Gallery

↓ **JACOB MARCH**
Tibetan Obsession 2011
Antique beads of turquoise, coral, agate, and pure gold. The eye bead (inset in clasp) known as "dZi", is revered by Tibetans as the most powerful mystical protection.
(Photo by Erin Dugan)

↑ **FARRESS CROMBE**
Northern Lights 2011
Bead embroidery using seed beads, fur, natural stick, and various goodies.
(Photo by Laura Crombe)

↑ **WENDY ELLSWORTH**
Shaman's Bag 1997
Bead embroidery, peyote stitch bezel using bison leather, seed beads, biggs jasper cabochon, silver conchos, dentalium shells, and deer antler buttons.
(Photo by David Ellsworth)

↓ RALONDA PATTERSON

Willow 2011

Bead embroidery and off-loom stitches using wire, wood, polymer clay, silk, and beads.

(Photo by Bradford Bosher)

↓ SUSAN ANNISKETT

Koi Fish 2011

Two-needle couching on felt using 10º–20º seed beads and black leather.

(Photo by Heidi Kummli)

↑ SUSAN ANNISKETT

Monarchs and Wild Geraniums 2011

Bead embroidery using couching method with size 10º–18º seed beads and black leather.

(Photo by Heidi Kummli)

← PAT DANIELS

In Memory of Raven 2011

Bead embroidery using seed beads, sequins, cabochons, lampwork, and porcelain raven by Laura Mears.

(Photo by the artist)

Resources

BEADS & SUPPLIES
Beyond Beadery
800-840-5548
beyondbeadery.com

Bead Lounge
303-678-9966
beadlounge.com

Fire Mountain Gems & Beads
800-355-2137
firemountaingems.com

Nomad Beads
303-786-9746
nomadbeads.com

Ornamental Resources Inc
800-876-6762
ornabead.com

CABOCHONS
Gary B. Wilson
520-877-1066
garywilsonstones.com

Zarlene Imports
800-233-7999
zarlene.com

FINDINGS
Designers Findings
262-574-1324
designerfindings.net

Rio Grande
800-545-6566
riogrande.com

ETSY SHOPS
etsy.com/shop/charmsgalore

etsy.com/shop/coolredwell

etsy.com/shop/dimestoreemporium

etsy.com/shop/patinaworx

ULTRASUEDE
Fields Fabrics
1695-44th Street, SE
Grand Rapids, MI 49508
616-455-9330
fieldsfabrics.com

PORCELAIN ANIMALS BY LAURA MEARS
Beyond Beads Gallery
509-891-8653
beyondbeads.com

SPIRITUAL READING AND LISTENING
Animal Speaks
by Ted Andrews
Llewellyn Publications

The Crystal Bible
by Judy Hall
Walking Stick Press

Medicine Cards
by Jamie Sams & David Carson
Bear & Company

Healing Crystals
by Cassandra Eason
Collins & Brown

A New Earth
by Eckhart Tolle
Namaste Publishing

Peace In Every Step
by Thich Nhat Hanh
Bantam Books

Rose Red Elk aka
Red Feather Woman
www.redfeatherwoman.com
rose@redfeatherwoman.com

Gallery Artists

Susan Anniskett
Port Charlotte, Florida
sanniskett@comcast.net

Frieda Bates
Carlsbad, New Mexico
fbates@pvtnetworks.net
pvtnetworks.net

Edda Blume
Pittsburgh, Pennsylvania
eddablume@yahoo.com
eddablume.com

Micheline Brierre
Colorado Springs, Colorado
mbrierre@michelinebrierre.com
michelinebrierre.com

Farress Crombe
Rochester, New York
farr23@bluefrog.com

Pat Daniels
Wheatridge, Colorado
Beadlab@aol.com

Alison Dearborn
Boulder, Colorado
alison@sacredcave.co
sacredcave.com

Margie Deeb
Roswell, Georgia
margie@margiedeeb.com
margiedeeb.com

Wendy Ellsworth
Quakertown, Pennsylvania
david.ellsworth3@gmail.com
ellsworthstudios.com

Janis Holler
Berthoud, Colorado
locolobo@earthlink.net
locolobodesigns.com

Diane Hyde
Brookfield, Wisconsin
dianehyde@mac.com
designersfindings.net

Laura Humenik
Longmont, Colorado
lhumenik1@msn.com
landsglory.com

Heidi Kummli
Nederland, Colorado
freespiritcollection.com
heidikummli@gmail.com

Jacob March
Boulder, Colorado
jake@nomadbeads.com

Ralonda Patterson
Decatur, Texas
ralonda_p@yahoo.com
beaded2bless.blogspot.com

JoAnn Patterson-Lavely
Littleton, Colorado
jopat@hotmail.com

Victoria Pearman
Carefree, Arizona
twobeadorknot@yahoo.com
artntheheart.blogspot.com

Sherry Serafini
Natrona Heights, Pennsylvania
sserafini1512@comcast.net
serafinibeadedjewelry.com

Janet Kay Skeen
Denver, Colorado
janet2planet@comcast.net
janet2planet.com

Photography Credits

Unless otherwise noted, all nature, animal, and step-by-step photos by Heidi Kummli.

Rose Red Elk, page 5,
Jim Barbour

Horses, page 29,
Rikki_/dreamstime.com

Fox, page 30,
Robbin Rawlings

Raven, page 31,
Svetlana Foote/dreamstime.com

Bobcat, page 32,
Tom Zaph

Cardinal, page 38,
Mirceax/dreamstime.com

Snake, page 43,
Paul Ransome/dreamstime.com

Fire, page 43,
Pjmorley/dreamstime.com

Water, page 44,
Alexey Rybakor/dreamstime.com

Fish, page 44,
Isselee/dreamstime.com

Lily, page 46,
Robbin Rawlings

Hummingbird, back cover,
© Barry D. Kaplan 2011

Thank you to my family and friends for your support and encouragement; I love you all. Thank you to my dogs over the years for taking me into nature everyday. Thank you Kalmbach Publishing Co. for again believing in my ideas and making them possible. You all are awesome to work with.

Thank you to all the wonderful people that buy my work and take my classes; you are my teachers, my gifts. Thanks to all the amazing artists that were willing to share their work for the gallery and bring beauty into this world. Thank you to my dear friend Sherry Serafini for sharing a beautiful project, writing the introduction for this book, and inspiring so many people. And thank you to Rose Red Elk for writing the beautiful story "Light Woman's Spirit Bead."

Thank you for my life situations and, yes, thank you to my cancer—if it weren't for you I would still be unconscious. My cancer is part of my path, my spiritual growth, my practice. It has opened my whole world.

Thank you great spirit for letting me be the experiencer of my life and for letting me listen to nature. Can you hear it?

Heidi F Kummli

Indulge yourself with more seed bead artistry...

The Art of Bead Embroidery
Heidi Kummli and Sherry Serafini share their advice about adhesives, materials, and techniques for 12 fabulous projects. Find inspiration for beautifully embroidered pieces of wearable art in a gorgeous gallery of their work.
62434 • $21.95

Beading Across America
Discover how the geographical regions of 30 accomplished artists influence their style. Each designer presents a unique piece of beadwork, shares the story behind it, and offers how-to instructions.
64001 • $21.95

Artistic Seed Bead Jewelry
Maggie Roschyk shows you how to translate inspirational sources into 13 stunning bead-stitched designs. Learn tips for choosing bead colors, how to "audition" your beads, and more.
64292 • $21.95